T0323745

Cambridge Elements ☰

Elements in Shakespeare and Pedagogy
edited by
Liam E. Semler
University of Sydney
Gillian Woods
Birkbeck College, University of London

CRITICAL PEDAGOGY AND ACTIVE APPROACHES TO TEACHING SHAKESPEARE

Jennifer Kitchen
University of Warwick

CAMBRIDGE
UNIVERSITY PRESS

CAMBRIDGE
UNIVERSITY PRESS

Shaftesbury Road, Cambridge CB2 8EA, United Kingdom

One Liberty Plaza, 20th Floor, New York, NY 10006, USA

477 Williamstown Road, Port Melbourne, VIC 3207, Australia

314–321, 3rd Floor, Plot 3, Splendor Forum, Jasola District Centre,
New Delhi – 110025, India

103 Penang Road, #05–06/07, Visioncrest Commercial, Singapore 238467

Cambridge University Press is part of Cambridge University Press & Assessment,
a department of the University of Cambridge.

We share the University's mission to contribute to society through the pursuit of
education, learning and research at the highest international levels of excellence.

www.cambridge.org
Information on this title: www.cambridge.org/9781108792653

DOI: 10.1017/9781108874656

First published 2023

A catalogue record for this publication is available from the British Library

ISBN 978-1-108-79265-3 Paperback
ISSN 2632-816X (online)
ISSN 2632-8151 (print)

Additional resources for this publication at www.cambridge.org/Kitchen.

Critical Pedagogy and Active Approaches to Teaching Shakespeare

Elements in Shakespeare and Pedagogy

DOI: 10.1017/9781108874656

First published online: November 2023

Jennifer Kitchen

University of Warwick

Author for correspondence: Jennifer Kitchen, jennifer.kitchen@warwick.ac.uk

ABSTRACT: Active approaches to teaching Shakespeare are growing in popularity, seen not only as enjoyable and accessible, but as an egalitarian and progressive teaching practice. A growing body of resources supports this work in classrooms. Yet critiques of these approaches argue they are not rigorous and do little to challenge the conservative status quo around Shakespeare. Meanwhile, Shakespeare scholarship more broadly is increasingly recognising the role of critical pedagogy, particularly feminist and decolonising approaches, and asks how best to teach Shakespeare within twenty-first-century understandings of cultural value and social justice. Via vignettes of schools' participation in Coram Shakespeare School Foundation's festival, this Element draws on critical theories of education, play and identity to argue active Shakespeare teaching is a playful co-construction with learners and holds rich potential towards furthering social justice–oriented approaches to teaching the plays.

KEYWORDS: Shakespeare, pedagogy, social justice, drama education, critical theory

ISBNs: 9781108792653 (PB), 9781108874656 (OC)
ISSNs: 2632-816X (online), 2632-8151 (print)

Contents

Introduction   1

1   Active Shakespeare as Critical Pedagogy   6

2   Critical Pedagogy: Core Principles   23

3   Playing as Reading the Text   35

4   Identity and Care in the Active Shakespeare Classroom   45

5   Critical Active Shakespeare as Restorying   61

References   70

Additional Online Practitioner Prompt Sheets are available at www.cambridge.org/Kitchen

Introduction

The key thesis of this Element is that teaching Shakespeare through active approaches is an act of critical pedagogy. In this Element, I use the term 'active Shakespeare' to refer to a range of practical, collaborative and drama-based approaches to teaching Shakespeare developed throughout the twentieth century and now increasingly championed by a range of Shakespeare-focused theatres, scholars and teaching practitioners (Banks 2014; Gibson 2016; Neelands & O'Hanlon 2011; O'Brien et al. 2006; Rocklin 2005; Stredder 2004; Winston 2015; Winston & Tandy 2012). Active Shakespeare literature and practice is often focused on work in schools and with school-aged children, but, within this Element, I include considerations of Shakespeare education in the broadest sense. 'Critical pedagogy' is defined here by 'resisting the harmful effects of dominant power' (Kincheloe 2008: 34) through education. Critical pedagogy is a multifaceted and diverse area of educational theory and practice (Cho 2016; Wink 2011), as I discuss in further detail in Section 2 of this Element. Ultimately, however, critical pedagogy is about teaching in ways which actively further social justice, not only for our specific students but also for society at large.

Issues of equitable and social justice–focused education are becoming ever more prevalent in drama education scholarship and practice, motivated by the increasingly inequitable and undemocratic nature of social, political and economic relations in many contexts across the globe (Freebody & Finneran 2021; Hughes & Nicholson 2016; Neelands 2010a, 2016; O'Connor & Anderson 2015; Thompson & Turchi 2020a). In recent years, these concerns have been informed by issues such as the global rise of populism, the continuing racial oppression which prompts the activism of the Black Lives Matter movement and the systemic acts of misogyny and gendered violence which fuel the #MeToo campaign. As Ayanna Thompson and Laura Turchi have argued, millennial and now 'Gen Z' students are hungry for engagement in social justice issues within their education (Thompson & Turchi 2020a, 2020b). Futurists, meanwhile, have emphasised the need for criticality, resilience, empathy and innovation within education in order to equip learners with the abilities to grapple with the 'massive systems change' of social and climate instability (Varaidzo 2019). Moreover, recent Shakespeare education and scholarship volumes demonstrate the growing engagement with social justice within Shakespeare studies specifically (Eklund & Hyman 2019; Ruiter 2020a). David Ruiter, editor of one such recent volume, writes of the intention to establish a 'field of play for the analysis and enactment of social justice via Shakespeare' (Ruiter 2020b: 1). In exploring the resonances between active Shakespeare teaching practice and social justice–focused critical pedagogy, this Element, therefore, aims to contribute to this growing field of play from a drama and theatre in education perspective.

As mentioned at the opening of this section, my claim in this is specific: claiming active Shakespeare teaching practice *as an act of critical pedagogy* is distinct from claiming that Shakespeare's works in and of themselves either inherently embody or can be *used for* social justice aims. The study of Shakespeare can and has been put to almost any curricular or pedagogic use you can imagine – the combination of rich source material and entrenched global cultural capital means Shakespeare is drawn on in the teaching of English language learning (Cheng & Winston 2011), zoology (MacFaul 2015), for corporate training (Shakespeare's Globe Theatre 2021), for citizenship (Lighthill 2011) and for yoga (Szabo-Cassella 2016). It is saying too little to claim Shakespeare can be used *for* social justice ends, therefore. But neither am I making a definitive claim that the works of Shakespeare themselves are inherently socially just. That would be saying too much. As Ruben Espinosa states, reflecting on Shakespeare as a potential lens to comprehend the racist extremism which fuelled the El Paso shooting in August 2019: 'Do we really need Shakespeare to understand this? My firm answer is: No. But I wholeheartedly believe that Shakespeare needs us. It is up to those of us committed to issues of social justice to locate in Shakespeare the moments that will allow for the candid and necessary discussions in our classrooms' (Espinosa 2019b)

This Element specifically focuses on the affordances of theatre-based active Shakespeare *pedagogy* and its potential to facilitate both the identification of social justice–focused moments in Shakespeare and the candid discussions that have been highlighted as essential by Espinosa. In terms of Shakespeare's texts themselves therefore, in this Element, I work from an understanding of their moral and social ambiguity. This is a quality which has been highlighted across Shakespeare scholarship, termed variously as the works' 'aspectuality' (Bate 1997: 327), their 'negative capability' (Keats, cited in Bate 1997: 330) to produce multiple and conflicting truths and their 'sheer and permissive gappiness' (Smith 2019a: 3).

The development of active Shakespeare across the twentieth century builds a pedagogy directly grounded in this 'aspectuality' and 'gappiness'. In doing so, the practice shares a series of educational and epistemological principles which are also the underlying building blocks of critical pedagogy. Taking this educational common ground as its starting point, the overarching argument of this Element is that when you explore that common pedagogic ground between active Shakespeare and critical pedagogies, you can unearth a variety of ways to make visible and extend the social justice potential of Shakespeare education.

I undertake this exploration as both a scholar and practitioner of active Shakespeare work. My core training as a practitioner was led by scholars deeply versed in ensemble pedagogy (Neelands 2009b, 2009a; Pigkou-Repousi 2012), in notions of theatre education as a collaborative and moral beauty (Winston 2005, 2010) and in understandings of theatre education as embedded in wider community spaces (Turner-King 2018). I brought these educational and aesthetic principles to my work as an educational Practitioner-in-Residence at Shakespeare's Globe, UK, where I led on local community education projects in the Globe's culturally diverse London borough of Southwark. Here, I engaged more deeply with how a theatre's spatial affordances and cultural history can inform educational work and was delighted to find resonances between my postgraduate training and historical readings of Shakespeare and his troupe of fellow actors as an ensemble (Banks 2014). In the inclusive and embodied tradition of active Shakespeare approaches, I focused on creating workshops and productions which aimed to make Shakespeare's texts and the historical theatre spaces engaging and accessible for global educational visitors. I struggled with how to make sense of occupying a space which spoke to the cultural reverence of Shakespeare as elite art, whilst simultaneously aiming to create an egalitarian space to explore these texts with diverse learners and creators. It was this sense-making struggle that led me back to academia, to explore the democratic and social justice claims of active 'ensemble' approaches to teaching Shakespeare (Neelands & O'Hanlon 2011) via a critical ethnography of a number of schools' participation in Coram Shakespeare Schools Foundation's (CSSF) festival project (Kitchen 2015, 2021).

This Element is, therefore, informed by the scholarly analysis and conclusions of this research as well as reflections on my creative and educational praxis. In particular, it has been prompted by a growing awareness of, and discomfort with, some of the deficit and paternalistic narratives surrounding the facilitation of active Shakespeare work in diverse and marginalised young communities. This growing realisation was significantly informed by a narrative I have repeatedly encountered from adults throughout my research and practice positioning EAL (English as an additional language) learners, working-class students and students of colour as suffering from an inherent cultural deficit. 'They never experience … *any* form of cultural experience' was a typical statement. From this premise was drawn the implication that Shakespeare was, therefore, first and foremost morally 'improving' for these students. As recent research has explored (Barnes 2020), in this narrative of encounters with Shakespeare being 'transformative' for diverse and marginalised young people, the empowerment of young people is the stated aim; yet, it is Shakespeare who is granted agency, that is, the power to catalyse transformation. Through witnessing these narratives, I had to allow that there was something in the critiques levelled against active Shakespeare approaches and that, far from being a force for inclusivity and social justice, they were in many ways actually perpetuating a conservative status quo by invoking the *idea* of active and egalitarian engagement with the texts, whilst still positioning students as culturally inferior and/or passive within that interaction. Yet, alongside this, I hold my own experiences of the reflexive, student- and care-led pedagogy of many active Shakespeare practitioners' work: an experience which tells me a more egalitarian active Shakespeare approach is possible. A growing increase in critical and social justice–focused scholarship across both Shakespeare and drama and theatre education, alongside a sense of the radical and emancipatory potential of such work, echoes these principles elsewhere (Eklund & Hyman 2019; Freebody & Finneran 2021; Gallagher et al. 2020; Ruiter 2020a).

It is from this discursive positionality of both commitment to and critique of my chosen area of scholarship and practice that I undertake this Element. After over a decade of practice and research, I am convinced of the critical and emancipatory value of active Shakespeare work and equally convinced that the field needs to do better to fully and rigorously realise this in a variety of contexts. Within this Element, I therefore set out a substantial argument for active Shakespeare as a critical pedagogy endeavour and in parallel develop a critical analysis explaining how this can be actioned in practice.

In Section 1, I set the theoretical and practical scene of the Element, mapping the core pedagogical conceits of active Shakespeare literature, their critical pedagogy potential and also the critiques they have encountered. I suggest there exists within active Shakespeare pedagogy and practice a tendency towards universalism with regard to Shakespeare's texts and their use in mainstream educational contexts. In Section 2, I further contextualise the theory and practice of critical pedagogy as a school of educational thought, in particular drawing out its long-standing connections with drama and theatre education practice. Section 3 explores how the pedagogy of play is thoroughly embedded in active Shakespeare literature and practice and the epistemological and social justice implications of this play-based pedagogy, while Section 4 focuses on care- and identity-led teaching practices within active Shakespeare teaching, highlighting both core examples of these practices and where they remain underdeveloped in the literature. In Section 5, I outline how the warp of playful text work and weft of learners' contextualised identities and knowledges can be woven into a critical and social justice–oriented 'restorying' (Dyches 2017) of the texts and explore the pedagogical and epistemological implications of this for future Shakespeare education work. It is through more deeply exploring and also problematising the relationship between these critical aspects of active Shakespeare pedagogy that I aim to reassert its value and potential as a social justice–oriented education practice.

The invitation to the reader through this exploration is to more deeply recognise and explore the active teaching of Shakespeare as critical pedagogy in your own teaching practice. This invitation is extended to teachers of all ages, and in the broadest of educational contexts, though many of the sources I cite are aimed at a UK school and higher education audience.

To complement this invitation within the text of the Element itself, I have curated a series of Online Practitioner Prompt Sheets to accompany Sections 2–5 (available to access at www.cambridge.org/kitchen). Each of these includes:

- A curated set of (open access) reading and resources
- At least one 'pedagogy prompt' to stimulate application of ideas in your own teaching context
- Links with some key exercises drawn from the active Shakespeare 'toolkit' literature
- Reflective prompts which may kindle further exploration of the ideas and practices introduced across this Element.

Like the Element itself, these are framed to speak to teachers and practitioners in the broadest sense, rather than any particular classroom context. As the name 'Online Practitioner Prompt Sheets' suggests, in the structuring and presentation of these resources, I have aimed to stay in the language of offers rather than instructions. I am delighted to have this opportunity to share some of the resources which have inspired my thinking and practice in these areas and I hope they are similarly stimulating for you, though they are in no way a collective formula or prescription.

1 Active Shakespeare as Critical Pedagogy

Setting the Scene

A drama class, aged 14–16, in an inner London secondary school is taking part in the CSSF festival project[1]. It is early in the rehearsal process, though the group has spent two weeks workshopping the play: exploring core themes through a variety of improvised physical exercises. The cast are scattered across the raked seating of their school's studio theatre space, undertaking a read-through of the text, a 30-minute edit of *Titus Andronicus*. The group has just reached the point where Titus' two sons have been falsely executed by the state, and his only daughter is returned

---

[1] https://static.shakespeareschools.org/

to him violated and mutilated. The director of this cast, class teacher Grace,[2] has paused the read-through and invited the group to summarise Titus' mental state at this point in the play, though the group has steered the discussion in the direction of its own interests in, and questions of, the text:

Shalini: I liked Lucius, it's all Titus' fault.

Grace: It's all Titus' fault?

Nami: It's not all Titus' fault.

Tapani: It sort of is.

Grace: Why it sort of is?

Tapani: Because, at the start, he kills his –

Jocelyn (from across the room): He kills her son.

Grace: But what has happened to his sons?

Tapani: They died in war.

Grace: By whose hand?

Tapani, Nami, Shalini, Saguna simultaneously: Tamora!

Grace: The Goths, Tamora's queen of the goths.

Saguna: So it's all Tamora's fault!

Grace: Is it?

Tapani: It's like half half, because they both want to get each other –

Nami (overlapping): But if Titus . . .

Grace: Yes, it's this whole cycle of revenge. If, if, what if –

Nami: Tamora's more evil than him.

Saguna: Yeah, Tamora's more evil than him.

Grace: But is she?

Tapani: I think they're the same.

Grace: He killed one of her sons, as she begged for mercy?

(Kitchen 2018: 192–3)

This is an extract from my doctoral research into active and collaborative approaches to teaching Shakespeare in schools. This class was my central

---

[2] Pseudonyms are used throughout for the research participants.

case study and I had the privilege of following its rehearsal process for the CSSF festival through the summer and autumn terms of 2014. The discussion is quick and lively; the students frequently talk across each other and Grace. The question about who is to blame for the events of the play is not one Grace has posed, but it is one Tapani, Saguna and Nami in particular are keen to explore. Grace holds back from imposing an interpretation, although she scaffolds and extends this discussion by introducing the theme of revenge and by short, open questions inviting the students to explore their perspectives based on specific details from the text. In this way, the students are prompted to both actively apply their knowledge of events in the play to justify their interpretations and to discuss these collaboratively in ways grounded in their own interests. Themes of the play, such as honour, blame and revenge, are attended to in ways that are explorative and unfinished. As teachers and practitioners, we can recognise the rich and creative learning which is happening within this exchange as the students enthusiastically engage in textual analysis as part of their preparations for performance. But we would probably also be aware, maybe less distinctively (for who prompts us to assess this?), of the empowering and collaborative social development which is occurring. The students are becoming confident in voicing their own opinions; open to listening to others' perspectives and comfortable with the ambiguity of these multiple ways into the text.

This extract is, for me, an excellent example of the pedagogical quality and educational value of active Shakespeare, that is, Shakespeare teaching and learning based on the core recognition of the plays as scripts for performance and thus grounded in the techniques and traditions of drama and theatre education. By 'techniques and traditions of theatre', I include close-text reading in ways that are active in their explorative, discursive and collaborative nature. Active Shakespeare is, therefore, not a static or narrow concept. As Shakespeare education scholars Ayanna Thompson and Laura Turchi observe: 'There are subtle and important distinctions between, and permeations of, active approaches (performance-based, rehearsal-room based, embodied, kinaesthetic and more). Nonetheless, they all have their roots in the blending of theatre and literary studies' (Thompson and Turchi 2020a: 52), and in this Element I take an expansive understanding of the term.

The exchange between Grace and her students in the aforementioned extract typifies the relationship between active Shakespeare and critical pedagogy. The teaching and learning are undertaken via a shared process of interpretation: the teacher frames the discussion and uses her understanding of the play and awareness of the educational outcomes she wants to develop; but nevertheless she leaves genuine space for the students' understandings and perspectives, ensuring the shared interpretation of the play developed within the class is active and collaborative. In addition to furthering their understanding of the play and developing their ideas for performance, the students are addressing core social questions of justice, blame and revenge. This can be read as critical pedagogy, that is, as an approach to teaching which is concerned with identifying and resisting social injustice, exclusion and oppression.

The central premise of this Element is that active Shakespeare and critical pedagogy share core educational assumptions, a combined theoretical starting point, which holds rich implications for those interested in teaching Shakespeare in more active and inclusive ways. These two theoretical assumptions are:

- Social constructivism: Knowledge and meaning as provisional and co-constructed.
- Progressivism: Learners as active and capable agents in their own learning.

Social constructivism can be defined as a theory of education which recognises knowledge as socially constructed. Built on the ideas of educational theorists such as Lev Vygotsky and Jerome Bruner (Bruner 2006; Vygotsky 1978), social constructivism emphasises the communal and collaborative nature of education as well as its active relationship to broader society and social norms. While progressivism can be understood as an educational theory developed around the work of nineteenth- and twentieth-century educational theorists such as John Dewey and building on the rationalist liberal view of Enlightenment scholars such as Jean-Jacques Rousseau (Dewey 1916; Rousseau 1762). Progressivism holds that learning is most effective when it is an active experience which recognises learners' existing knowledge and capacity.

*Active Shakespeare as Critical Pedagogy: The Educational
Implications of the Text as Script*

In the 1980s, education academic Rex Gibson began the Shakespeare in
Schools Project at Cambridge University, working in collaboration with
schoolteachers nationally to explore and develop active approaches to
teaching Shakespeare (Irish 2008). These explorations informed a series
of newsletters produced during the project's lifetime, the Cambridge
University Press 'School Shakespeare' editions of the plays with accompanying suggestions for teaching and performance and the 1998 book
Teaching Shakespeare. While also being one of the most recognisable of
the active Shakespeare handbooks or 'toolkits', *Teaching Shakespeare* is
moreover a collation of many years' worth of practice and exploration
from a variety of teachers across the UK. This foundational work joined
both a long-term educational interest in active and performative approaches
to teaching Shakespeare within the UK (Caldwell Cook 1917; Finlay-
Johnson 1912; Irish 2008) and parallel discourses in the US and Australian
education contexts (Flaherty et al. 2013; O'Brien et al. 2006; Rocklin 2005).
By exploring the rationale for the active teaching of Shakespeare laid out in
Teaching Shakespeare, it is possible to identify the two core critical pedagogy assumptions of active Shakespeare. The linchpin of these two assumptions is Gibson's overriding premise 'that Shakespeare wrote his plays for
performance, and that his scripts are completed by enactment of some kind'
(Gibson 2016: viii).

This is at the core of Gibson's active approach: viewing Shakespeare's
plays as scripts, that is, not only usefully and enjoyably engaged with
through performance, but actually completed and given full meaning in
this way. While the terminology of this assertion varies across Shakespeare
education literature, with some using the word 'texts' to define these
potential-laden, incomplete documents and 'scripts' for any final adaptation
or performance (Dawson 2009), the implications are the same: the plays are
not singular, inert packages of meaning but are brought into full being via
active interpretation. This ontological starting point echoes across active
Shakespeare literature, for example, when James Stredder states 'The text is
treated as a script, a score for performance, a huge store of works to be taken

out and used, a field for play and experiments' (Stredder 2004: 13). In the active Shakespeare understanding of the plays as scripts, there is a definition of knowledge as ultimately unfinished and up for interpretation. This chimes both with Shakespearean scholars who have highlighted the messy multiplicity in his plays (Bate 1997) and with broader interpretive literary theories which see meaning in all texts as provisional and as actively constructed in through the process of reading. This perspective also holds a key social implication: the 'knowledges' and norms of our society are not inherent or static but actively interpreted and constructed over time, as is acknowledged in recent works exploring Shakespeare and social justice (Eklund & Hyman 2019; Ruiter 2020a).

If knowledge or meaning is always provisional and requiring interpretation, then it follows that the individuals or groups who are undertaking that interpretation – that is, learners – are active agents within, not passive recipients of, that knowledge. This is the second core principle shared by active Shakespeare and critical pedagogies. As Gibson has it: 'Through such participatory and co-operative activity, students both discover and create meaning. They become agents of their own learning as they take responsibility for their own inquiries and investigations' (Gibson 2016: vii). This principle will be familiar to anyone who has experience with the ideas of progressive and experiential education. There is a basic precept of the learner as having an inherent capacity for learning and as bringing their existing knowledges to the classroom (Greene 1987). Within this, a good education is understood as 'authentic' learning experiences which draw on learners' capacity and which are relevant to their existing knowledges (Dewey 1916). There is a range of cultural implications within these educational perspectives of social constructivism and progressivism. Again turning to Gibson: 'The recognition that learners actively *make* meaning has cultural implications. Each student brings their own culture to every lesson. That rich variety of culture is a resource that Shakespeare lessons can celebrate and employ rather than dismiss' (Gibson 2016: 10).

These core precepts of active Shakespeare, based around the understanding of the plays as scripts, therefore, do not merely *support* the inclusion and development of students' diverse readings of Shakespeare;

they *require* it in order for the approach to function. Accessible, relevant and culturally diverse readings of Shakespeare are not a welcome side effect of active Shakespeare, but they are centrally necessary for this way of teaching and learning the plays. Active Shakespeare, therefore, goes beyond a learner's individual and personal interaction with Shakespeare, though this is an important aspect. Because the knowledge of the plays is provisional and the existing perspectives the students bring are valuable, it follows both that this active meaning making is most effective as a collaborative endeavour and that the wider community and cultural contexts in which the learning is occurring are centrally relevant. Gibson argues throughout his book that the individual learner's reactions to the play should not be treated in 'overly romantic and personal' terms (Gibson 2016: 9) but rather as a starting point for shared, multiple and unfixed interpretations of the plays. Crucially, he emphasises how these dynamic and collaborative interpretive processes directly link to, and facilitate the exploration of, the issues and questions Shakespeare poses to us as a society.

So, while Gibson does focus on how the content of the plays – what he terms each of their 'distinctive qualities' – prompts engagement in particular social justice issues (Gibson 2016: 18), what is emphasised here is that there is a more inherent pedagogic commitment to social justice in the assumptions active Shakespeare holds about the nature of knowledge and the capacity of learners. This commitment to social justice is built, therefore, not on any one position or theme of Shakespeare's plays themselves but draws on their *lack* of single cohesive viewpoint. It is precisely their messy, open-ended and sometimes directly troubling plurality which prompts Gibson's treatment of them as working 'scripts' rather than finalised 'texts' (Gibson 2016: 8).

Stredder argues for the synergy between collaborative, embodied action and critical textual analysis inherent in the active Shakespeare premise of the plays as scripts:

> This notion of producing or 'making' the characters or the
> narrative of a play is attractive, both to progressive pedagogy (it
> is creative, stimulating, participatory, offers ownership) and to
> the rigours of modern critical theory (where meaning is actively
> produced by reader/audience and situation, rather than

> universal or inherent ...). Taken together, these progressive
> and critical emphases set up a learner-centred and text-centred
> base for active work, which is invaluable to teachers.
> (Stredder 2004: 12)

Stredder terms this fortuitous combination of learner- and text-centred approaches he finds within active Shakespeare a 'new progressivism' and emphasises its value not only as a workable and engaging approach to teaching the plays but also as a way to actively combat what he terms the prevalent monumentalism of Shakespeare: 'an aura bestowed by culture and history, a feeling of immoderate respect, that can make people snobbishly subservient or cowed and resentful' (Stredder 2004: 7). As Hillary Eklund and Wendy Hyman summarise in their edited volume *Teaching Social Justice through Shakespeare*, 'social change and pedagogy are baked into dramatic form itself. The study and teaching of plays, therefore, afford a clear opportunity to engage in conversations about social justice' (Eklund & Hyman 2019: 8).

Active Shakespeare as Critical Pedagogy: Democratic Cultural Entitlement

Alongside this pedagogic proposition of active Shakespeare as inherently constructivist and progressive, there exists within active Shakespeare literature and practice a conscious commitment to democratic cultural citizenship. This occurs within the literature and resources via a commitment of 'universal access' to Shakespeare and through an appreciation of the rich democratic potential of ensemble theatre and drama principles related to active practice.

This can be seen in Gibson's emphasis on the 'emancipatory principle' of active Shakespeare, arguing that it establishes 'a clear democratic entitlement for all students to study Shakespeare, but also a democratic responsibility to understand other points of view, the "other-sidedness of things"', and to question 'what societies are or might be' (cited in Irish 2016: 96). Drama education practitioner and scholar Jonothan Neelands has perhaps argued most directly for this connection between social justice and active

approaches to teaching Shakespeare through his work on ensemble pedagogy in partnership with the Royal Shakespeare Company (RSC). Drawing
from the then Artistic Director Michael Boyd's proposition, 'Can an
ensemble ... act in some sense as a ... better version of the real world
on an achievable scale which celebrates the virtues of collaboration?'
(Equity and Directors Guild of Great Britain, 2004), Neelands and colleagues articulated a model of collaborative drama teaching based on the
rehearsal practices they observed during their work with Boyd's ensemble
casts. This presented the notion of ensemble pedagogy as a 'bridging
metaphor' for a variety of drama and progressive education ideals. In
Neelands' writings, ensemble pedagogy is a democratic model of teaching
in which learning to 'act together' in theatrical terms in the classroom
establishes a greater potential to 'act together' in civic terms in the wider
world (Monk et al. 2011b; Neelands 2009a; Neelands & O'Hanlon 2011). In
the ensemble-focused active Shakespeare writing of Neelands and colleagues, the value of this collaborative acting is seen as catalysed by
Shakespeare's rich and ambiguous language:

> At the heart of the RSC project there is critical hope in the
> power of collective human agency to make a difference to the
> world. Children and young people are encouraged through
> practical discovery and skilful questioning to make their
> own 'interpretive choices', as actors, about how to play
> Shakespeare's language. They learn that his texts are provi-
> sional and open to interpretation and that they can 'change' the
> playing of the play through their choices. There is here the
> hope that they may also learn that they can make interpretative
> choices in the wider world as well, including choices about who
> they might become or how the world might be re-imagined.
> (Neelands & O'Hanlon 2011: 284)

Neelands and O'Hanlon's description here foregrounds the social justice
focus of active Shakespeare teaching and articulates a vision which chimes
with many teachers who engage in these approaches. As drama education
scholar Peter O'Connor observed, for those researching and practicing in

this field, a belief in the social justice potential of ensemble pedagogy is 'rooted in the soul of humanity'(O'Connor in Neelands 2010b: 117). Active Shakespeare as a body of practice articulated through the writings of Gibson, Stredder, Neelands and many others is, therefore, not understood merely in terms of educational convenience or efficiency; it is an expression of the value and purpose of Shakespeare education. Through the constructivist and progressive pedagogic foundations it is grounded in, and the educational values it is aligned with, active Shakespeare can, therefore, be understood as a direct expression of critical pedagogy principles.

Here is the Rub: Universalism and Domestication

As active Shakespeare approaches have grown in popularity, so have their critiques. Shakespearean education scholar Sarah Olive, for example, argues that far from dethroning models of Shakespeare as exclusionary high culture, there is actually a link between active approaches and a perpetuation of Shakespeare as a 'natural' object of high culture (Olive 2011). Olive argues this via a critique of the active Shakespeare teaching approaches of the RSC in particular, suggesting that in promoting active approaches to teaching and consuming Shakespeare, organisations such as the RSC are conflating the particular value systems of these institutions with the values of Shakespeare him/itself. Olive suggests that for all of the surrounding rhetoric of democracy, this can ultimately be read as an appeasement of the conservative establishment: framed by an uncritical application of government-sanctioned curriculum outcomes couched in a rhetoric of 'faux-progressivism' (Olive 2011). Education scholar Jane Coles makes similar points speaking to 'active' and 'accessible' Shakespeare approaches in schools when she argues that these approaches, while drawing on well-meaning readings of Shakespeare's universal appeal and of young people's cultural entitlement to his works, combine with the high-stakes testing regimes of the UK schooling to similarly perpetuate an uncritical reproduction of oppressive norms of cultural dominance (Coles 2013). Shakespearean scholar Kate McLuskie makes a more fundamental pedagogical argument that embodied approaches in and of themselves foreshorten critical engagement with the texts (McLuskie 2009). Active Shakespeare has, therefore, been criticised both for perceived inherent shortcomings and a lack of effectiveness on its own terms in wider educational and cultural contexts. Shakespearean scholars and educators Ayanna Thompson and Laura Turchi's commentary on active Shakespeare's social justice claims offers a key explanation for these lines of critique when they suggest: While many proponents of active approaches to teaching Shakespeare are incredibly precise when it comes to myriad performance-based exercises (small group, large group, vocal, language, movement, etc.), when it comes to moments of racism, anti-Semitism, misogyny, etc. in the plays, they often leave matters rather vague' (Thompson and Turchi 2020a: 54)

They go on to argue that, while the literature surrounding active approaches nominally celebrates plurality, the learner is still treated in generalised terms in these texts, with too little consideration of their contextualised identity, limiting any potential social justice impact of the work.

There have been well-argued rebuttals of some of the more general claims of these arguments, stating that these critiques fail to acknowledge the pedagogic and practice-grounded basis for this work (Irish 2016) and focus on analysing promotional, public- and funder-facing policy documents, which could be argued to make core points in more generalised and accessible ways (Winston 2015). I would furthermore argue that they fail to acknowledge the broader interdisciplinary, creative and professional nexus in which active Shakespeare sits. Firstly, the critiques do not substantially engage with the scholarship of applied and educational drama and theatre, which offers rich theoretical and empirical exploration of the knotty questions of how and why drama and Shakespeare are taught in schools, universities and communities (Anderson & Dunn 2013; Bolton 1998; Finneran & Freebody 2016; Fleming 2010; Freebody et al. 2018; Gallagher 2017; Hornbrook 1998; Hughes & Nicholson 2016; Nicholson 2011). Furthermore, within these active Shakespeare critiques, there is little acknowledgement of the complex and contested relationship of traditional scholarship and creative practice within the field of applied and educational drama. In the early days of applied and educational drama as a field of scholarship, this relationship was initially defined by a sense of tension and resistance within the field to formal academic theory from reflective practitioners who were just beginning to move into university teaching and research posts in the mid- to late-twentieth century (Courtney 1990; O'Toole 2010). This developed towards carefully navigated research collaborations – and compromises – with educational and professional commercial partners (Winston 2015) by the later twentieth and early twenty-first centuries and to the continuing practice-focused, creative and multi-modal scholarship of the present day. In this field, therefore, equal weight is placed on practical and embodied work presented in workshops and masterclasses, which does not hold the archival permanence of written publications. For example, Thompson and Turchi state an awareness of the contextualised nature of learners' identities and culturally contingent gestures is not acknowledged within active Shakespeare practice (Thompson & Turchi 2020a: 56). However, several sessions of my own postgraduate training with active Shakespeare advocates Neelands and Winston focused on this very issue, using a combination of ensemble games and explorative exercises on the contingent nature of theatre semiotics in different cultural contexts. Likewise, in many years of supervising practicing teachers' postgraduate work on active Shakespeare, I have encountered dissertations explicitly focused on the implications of delivering these practices with diverse learners in international school communities, with special educational needs students, and in private school settings. Active Shakespeare is a diverse and evolving ecology of practice and scholarship, the nuances of which are not always acknowledged in these critiques.

With this Element, however, I acknowledge and utilise these critiques of active Shakespeare as a point of departure to critically re-examine and re-articulate the social justice potential of this teaching approach. In the remainder of this section, I begin this analysis by exploring the mechanics by which active Shakespeare literature and practice can indeed foreshorten and even undermine its own stated commitment to social justice. As Harry McCarthy highlights in his exploration of white allyship in relation to Shakespearean and early modern race scholarship (McCarthy 2021), active Shakespeare practitioners and scholars likewise need to acknowledge where our privileges – whether via whiteness, heteronormativity, maleness, cisgenderness or lack of marginalisation through class, religion, disability or neurodivergence – have prevented us from recognising where we maintain and reproduce the problems of imperialism, racism, sexism, homophobia, classism and other prejudices within and around Shakespeare's texts in our teaching practice and research.

The nature of this unwitting reproduction can be demonstrated by an analysis of Gibson's treatment of critical pedagogy and theory in *Teaching Shakespeare*. On the one hand, he celebrates throughout the text the necessity for a collaborative and constructivist approach to knowledge production, as discussed earlier. Likewise, he emphasises the potential for active Shakespeare approaches to foreground students' diverse and personalised interpretations of Shakespeare, arguing for this as an 'emancipatory principle' of the approach. Gibson argues that active Shakespeare practice facilitates students' democratic entitlement to engage in Shakespeare on their own terms. While, furthermore, it is through an embodied experience of the rich and ambiguous language that students can explore the 'othersidedness of things' and develop a critical perspective on 'what societies are and might be' (Irish 2016: 96). Yet, in *Teaching Shakespeare*, Gibson also maintains a lukewarm perspective on *literary* critical theory, a distinct body of scholarship from critical pedagogy, though related in its use of critical social theory as an analytic lens. Within the chapter 'Perspectives', Gibson gives an introduction to the principles of critical literary theory and lays out some key areas which have informed Shakespeare scholarship, including feminism, new historicism and cultural materialism, all of which can be said to chime with a critical pedagogy lens in their commitment to grounding understandings of the texts in terms of their socially contextualised and emancipatory potential. Notably absent from these perspectives, however, is anything approaching critical race theory, despite its growing influence by the 1990s (Hall 1995, 1998; Loomba 1989; McCarthy 2021). Gibson's inclusion of these theoretical perspectives does speak of a recognition of their relevance to active Shakespeare work, compared, for example, to Shakespeare's Globe and RSC teacher toolkit resources, which make minimal reference to critical theory of any kind (Banks 2014; Royal Shakespeare Company 2010). However, ultimately, Gibson remains sceptical of the agenda of these critical approaches as imposing analytic lenses on learner, failing to recognise how feminist or critical race readings of Shakespeare could equally arise from learners' experiences, knowledges and identities as from external, academic sources. The implied student of the student-led practices is, therefore, positioned as essentially de-politicised within *Teaching Shakespeare*.

I argue that there are two main ways in which active Shakespeare literature and resources engage in the de-politicisation of the principles of collaborative, student-led approaches highlighted here: (1) a commitment to the concept of universalism with regard to Shakespeare's cultural and educational value; (2) a process of 'domesticating' the critical pedagogy potential of active Shakespeare to remain palatable within mainstream contexts. Universalism can be understood as claiming the specific cultural and historical perspectives of the text as indicative of 'universal' ideas and values of humanity. Claims of Shakespeare's universalism are regularly made within active Shakespeare texts in support of their relevance and accessibility: 'Shakespeare really does deal in universals' (Gibson 2016: 16); 'They [the plays] are universal stories . . . timeless' (Banks 2014: 10). It is a recognisable assertion which makes a simple and powerful statement about the value and accessibility of Shakespeare's texts. However, it is also an inherently problematic claim as many critical Shakespearean scholars have explored. Firstly because it ignores the reality of the playtexts as products of a particular historical and cultural positionality (Thompson 2011); one which found amusement in, for example, the deliberate and systemised tormenting of a new wife (*The Taming of The Shrew*) and the downfall of a Jewish money lender (*The Merchant of Venice*). And secondly because it ignores the history of white, European imperialism and cultural supremacy (Eklund & Hyman 2019) which has informed, if not defined, the 400-year cultural history of Shakespeare's works. As Thompson and Turchi argue, we need to recognise undertaking Shakespeare teaching under a guide of 'universality' rings increasingly false with our students and is actively triggering to those who experience exclusion and oppression due to their race, class, gender or sexuality (Thompson & Turchi 2020b).

The notion of a universal Shakespeare, moreover, is in conflict with the core active Shakespeare premise of the plays as scripts. The playtexts cannot both require active interpretation for completion *and* be infinite fonts of humanity. Taking issue with claims of universalism is not about refuting the linguistic richness, aesthetic value or human complexity of the texts but about being conscious of and specific about the directions of cultural travel we are charting when we talk about the active and collaborative interpretation of those rich and complex texts. It is not a one-way process, with the Shakespearean texts as an endless cornucopia and readers/performers/audiences as industrious extractors of any one particular interpretation. It is about recognising the two-way process, in fact the dynamic multi-lane cultural interchange, which is occurring in any reading or performing of the texts; an interchange which is *equally* informed by the knowledges and positionalities of the readers as the rich potentiality of the text. In framing Shakespeare as a timeless, omniscient cornucopia, we are erasing the labour of diverse cultures and communities which perform, appropriate and adapt his work (Julian & Solga 2021). The claims of 'universality' are maintained directly on the backs of this labour and it is the diverse processes of interpretation and performance themselves which must be analysed and celebrated. For these reasons, despite the initial sense of validity and even inclusivity which comes from claims of universality, it is an insufficient concept which obscures the need to problematise the content and history of Shakespearean texts and to celebrate the multiple opportunities inherent in active interpretation of the plays as scripts. As Thompson and Turchi assert: 'This does not mean we value Shakespeare's text any less because we reject facile claims about their universality; rather the text's value comes in the rich and fascinating juxtaposition of histories, contexts, rhetoric and aesthetic theories' (Thompson & Turchi 2016: 49)

Domestication (Kitchen 2015; Neelands 2004), meanwhile, can be understood as the process of critical, creative and progressive education approaches being 'tamed' and standardised within existing metrics of mainstream schooling. It is a phenomenon which has similarly been observed of the social justice–focused performance techniques of Forum Theatre as they become commercialised and applied in educational and corporate contexts and thus separated from their original function as an arena for generative social change (Bala & Albacan 2013; Snyder-Young 2013). A 2010 evaluation report into the then flagship RSC ensemble school partnership project, the Learning Performance Network (LPN), charts the process of domestication with regard to active Shakespeare when it notes differences in focus and framing of teachers who worked directly with RSC practitioners – in 'core' schools – and those in 'cluster' schools who worked directly only with their 'core' school counterparts. The report observed, alongside many positive outcomes, that while finite and measurable results of involvement with the LPN, such as increased knowledge of Shakespeare plots and vocabulary and performance skills, continued to be valued by teachers in the 'cluster' schools, what faded was a commitment to the pro-social value of active Shakespeare which had been emphasised in the initial RSC and core school sessions (Thomson et al. 2010: 26). Furthermore, the ensemble sense of the rehearsal text as something actively and collaboratively interpreted over time was more limited or absent in some cluster schools (Thomson et al. 2010: 26).

This metrification is one branch of domestication. A parallel outcome of this pressure to translate the processes of active Shakespeare and similar creative and critical educational approaches into the positivistic language of interventions and outcomes is that the rhetorics of social justice, inclusion and democratic engagement are rendered 'miraculous' or mythologised (Finneran 2008; Neelands 2004). This rhetoric of the miraculous is demonstrated in the following 2014 quote from CSSF's website:

> The power of theatre to change the lives of young people who take part is familiar to any drama teacher. When you add the greatest genius of the stage and give children the chance to inhabit his immense characters and dramatic situations in a setting where the highest professional standards are a matter of daily practice, *the result is almost miraculous.*
> (Pullman 2014, emphasis mine)

This statement, which was posted alongside a range of inspiring stories of students' dramatic improvements in educational outcomes, confidence and articulation as a result of participation in the project, demonstrates how active Shakespeare pedagogy, divorced from its grounding in social constructivist and progressive educational principles, becomes 'magical' in its outcomes.

These two branches – the metric and the miracle – taken together therefore represent a process of domestication which ignores the risky and critical nature of active Shakespeare and erases the more radical social and epistemological elements of its pedagogic legacy. Thus, the results seem 'miraculous' in addition to being finite, measurable and predictable. This, firstly, misrepresents both the opportunities and challenges of the approach to teachers. Secondly, this domestication obscures and thus constrains the critical pedagogy potential of active Shakespeare, as it becomes positioned as just another intervention to be fed into the 'black box' (Delamont, 2014) of normative educational practice.

I would argue that recognising and naming these tendencies – which are not unique to the active teaching of Shakespeare but shared by all varieties of critical, creative and innovative teaching methods – is the necessary first step in becoming more consciously social justice–oriented in our active teaching of Shakespeare. Critical pedagogue Paulo Freire would call this a process of 'conscientisation': the critical consciousness raising practice of educators recognising and unlearning limiting models from the normative status quo (Freire 1972). By being more conscious of the critical pedagogy quality of active Shakespeare and its social justice potential, we can more robustly recognise and resist narratives of universalism and domestication in our work and practice. In doing this, I suggest we can become better critical pedagogues, more actively committed to fighting oppressive norms both within cultural discourse in more general terms and specifically in our education institutions with and for our students.

In this opening section, I have laid out my argument for the shared education principles of active Shakespeare and critical pedagogy. I have acknowledged the critiques of active Shakespeare and from these critiques explored how the tendency to perpetuate universalistic notions of Shakespeare's cultural value and domesticate active pedagogy in mainstream educational settings limits the social justice potential of active Shakespeare practice. To summarise: 'The mere fact of being collaborative, or participatory, or interactive is not enough to legitimize a work or guarantee its significance. It is more important to observe how it addresses – and intervenes in – the dominant conventions and relations of its time (Roche 2007)' (cited in Harvie 2011). In the following section, I therefore turn to critical pedagogy principles in more detail, to begin to explore how these limitations can be redressed and the critical social justice promise of active Shakespeare can be more fully explored in scholarship and realised in practice.

2 Critical Pedagogy: Core Principles

Critical pedagogy can be understood as an approach to education based on the belief that the current norms of our society are oppressive, the hope that a more equitable normality is possible and the conviction that education is a key arena in which to build that equitable normality. Critical pedagogy is, therefore, about teaching in ways which actively further social justice, not only for our specific students but also for society at large. In this section, I will explore in more depth the scholarly and professional history of the term, give a reflexive account of my own journey towards critical pedagogy as a theatre education practitioner and scholar and introduce the core critical pedagogy concepts relevant to understanding its relationship to active Shakespeare teaching.

In many ways, critical pedagogy is not a novel or clearly defined concept; it builds on and intersects with a wide variety of progressive, civil rights- and social justice–focused educational aims from the early twentieth century onwards (Cho 2016). It encompasses the work of feminist, post-colonialist, anti-racist and queer education scholars and practitioners (de Jong et al. 2019; Freire 1972; hooks 1994; Mayo & Rodriguez 2019) all of whom share a basic perspective that society at large is unjust by some measure and that the role of schools is, therefore, not to socialise students to maintain this society but to provide skills to *recognise* these injustices and *actively change* them for the better. It is from this broad base that the two core principles I identified in Section 1 have become central within critical pedagogy. The progressivist commitment to learners' existing knowledges and essential capacity and the social constructivist understanding of knowledge are both foundational in articulating a pedagogic process committed to revealing and dismantling unjust societal norms. Critical pedagogy, as enacted within the classroom, can therefore be understood as an approach which centralises young people, their knowledges, identities and experiences and deconstructs existing 'taken for granted' information and norms.

Critical approaches to education have coined a variety of phrases and concepts to identify these oppressive and 'taken for granted' norms. Freire, for example, speaks of the 'banking' model of education, where learners are seen as 'empty vessels' into which knowledge is to be poured (Freire 1972). This has also been termed the deficit model or medical model (Hargreaves 1997; Holligan 2010; Thomas 2009; Wright 2012). Finnish education writer Pasi Sahlberg most evocatively terms the growing homogenous commitment to these reductive models the Global Educational Reform Movement, or GERM, defined by a focus on 'competition between schools, standardization of teaching and learning, punitive test-based accountability, ill-informed performance-based pay, and data-driven decision making' (Sahlberg 2014: 142).

Critical pedagogy as a scholarly and professional concept can be said to stem from a group of primarily American educationalists researching and practicing from the 1970s onwards. Initially, these critical pedagogues came from a background in neo-Marxist critical theory and were interested in how they could move from the often deterministic and pessimistic conclusions on education within neo-Marxism to more hopeful and practice-engaged educational and scholarly work (Giroux 1997). In undertaking this, critical pedagogy scholars became strongly influenced by the Brazilian educationalist Paulo Freire (Freire 1972, 2000), whose pioneering literacy education work and accompanying publications offered a dynamic, practice-focused realisation of their theories, in particular through his focus on hope, 'conscientisation' and praxis, that is, 'theorizing practice and practicing theory' (Monchinski 2008: 1).

These initial 'classic' critical pedagogy perspectives, built directly as they were on a class-focused neo-Marxist analysis of education, were criticised and developed by feminist and critical race theory scholars, who highlighted the lack of focus given to the intersecting oppressions and injustices of misogyny, racism and colonialism within this first wave of critical pedagogy texts (Allen 2004; Ellsworth 1989; Leonardo 2002; Luke 1992). It is these more intersectional perspectives on critical pedagogy (de Jong et al. 2019; hooks 1994) that I aim to apply throughout this Element. As I have explored elsewhere (Kitchen 2021), there is specifically within critical drama and theatre pedagogy research a focus on feminist perspectives for the student-centred and discursive pedagogic frameworks they offer (Gallagher 2016a; Grady 2003).

Apart from these scholarly debates and explorations, critical pedagogy has been criticised on broader terms within education for being abstract, jargonistic and removed from the daily concerns and pressures of classroom practice. There are also criticisms that, as an overtly 'political' approach to education, critical pedagogy is too radical and partisan to be engaged with as a holistic approach to classroom teaching (Monchinski 2008: xiv). To respond to these critiques: there is firstly a difference between jargon and specificity. While it is undeniable that some critical pedagogy scholars make little apparent effort to be understood by a professional teaching or general public audience, there is also the need to recognise critical pedagogy is consciously working against the naturalised 'norms' of knowledge. Therefore, a shared terminology, sometimes highly specific or formalised, is needed to make visible and actively resist naturalised knowledge forms and the oppressions they reinforce. At its best, critical pedagogy scholarship and practice draws from rich and nuanced springs of critical social, feminist, queer and race theories in order to be able to name and change oppressive practices in schools and society more broadly through daily, practical processes. As I explore in the following, critical pedagogy theory is grounded in practice and individual reflexivity over time; not buy-in to any abstract, totalising theory, terminology or party-political allegiance.

I have come to these understandings on critical pedagogy through the lens of theatre education. As I discussed in the introductory section of this Element, after starting my career as a theatre education practitioner, I moved into research to explore more deeply the values and benefits of theatre education and, in particular, active approaches to teaching Shakespeare. As a doctoral candidate, I did not set out to write a thesis about social justice or critical pedagogy; I thought I was writing one about playfulness and collaboration. But, as is the way of these things, my research took me sharply in this direction and I had to catch up. I am not a classically trained critical theorist or educational sociologist; my understanding of critical pedagogy was developed on the hoof, as I grabbed at ideas and concepts to help me articulate what I was finding in my research data and what I understood from my own teaching experiences. This route through critical pedagogy was messy, partial and subjective, spiralling outwards from the critically engaged drama and theatre education scholars whose work I admired (Etheridge Woodson 2015; Finneran & Freebody 2016; Gallagher 2016b; Grady 2003; Hornbrook 1998; Hughes & Nicholson 2016; Neelands 2009a; Winston 2005). I share this context to emphasise that such partial and personalised approaches are an inherent quality of engaged critical pedagogy practice. If the aim of critical pedagogy is to make visible and disrupt oppressive social hegemonies, it stands to reason that the place we can most readily start is by making visible our own social and intellectual positionalities, recognising this not as bias to be reduced but as unavoidable subjectivities to work from and sometimes against. This is what drives the reflexive, ongoing educational processes of 'conscientisation', praxis and hope which are core to critical pedagogy.

Drama Education and Critical Pedagogy

Drama education as a field of study and practice has a long-standing affinity with critical pedagogy and concerns of social justice. As applied and educational theatre scholar Helen Nicholson has charted, from the nine-teenth century onwards, social reformers have connected engagement with the performing arts with social empowerment, albeit initially more focused on the 'civilising' quality of 'high' art and culture (Nicholson 2011). Within the early twentieth century, burgeoning ideas on child development, pro-gressive education and the beginnings of childhood play research informed foundational texts on the use of drama as a subject and mode of education in schools. Sussex schoolteacher Harriet Finley-Johnson, for example, wrote at the turn of the twentieth century of playful, drama-led teaching as a 'natural' pedagogy fostering self-regulation, interdependence and social and moral improvement in her rural working-class pupils (Finlay-Johnson 1912). Her contemporary Henry Caldwell Cook meanwhile, teaching at a middle-class Cambridgeshire boys' school, echoed similar sentiments with a more overtly social focus when he spoke of drama-centric classrooms as 'little republics' and described them as an 'essential moral training ground for the gentlemen of the future' (Caldwell Cook 1917: 96).

This early preoccupation in drama with the resonances between 'natural' child-led play, the 'civilising' potential of performance and progressive education continued throughout the twentieth century, notably via Brian

Way and Peter Slade's explorations of 'Child Drama' as a distinct – and educationally and culturally significant – art form (Slade 1954; Way 1967). Meanwhile, discourses of drama and social justice more concerned with radical and emancipatory aims developed via the influence of practices derived from German playwright and dramaturg Bertolt Brecht's Epic Theatre (Neelands 2010c) and the UK director Joan Littlewood's foundational work in working-class, community and youth theatre (Holdsworth 2007). Perhaps most significantly in terms of critical pedagogy is the work of Brazilian performer and director Augusto Boal, who worked closely with founding critical pedagogue Freire from the 1970s onwards, making connections between the educational and the performative within the search for emancipation and radical social change (Boal 2006). Boal developed and popularised the use of 'forum theatre' and 'image theatre': collaborative, processional performance practices designed to identify and counteract societal oppression. These liberal and radical social discourses continued to run through applied and educational drama and theatre (Gallagher et al. 2017) encompassing the improvisational 'living through' practices of process drama (Bolton 1986; Bowell & Heap 2001) through to the more performance-led work of theatre in education (Hughes & Nicholson 2016) with a rich tapestry in between.

A critical and social justice focus is arguably one of the most prominent themes of enquiry in contemporary applied and educational drama scholarship. While explicitly critical pedagogy-informed scholarship in this field is not a recent development (Grady 2003), it is becoming increasingly prominent across theatre and drama education literature (Adams Jr 2013; O'Connor 2014, 2016). Gallagher, often in collaboration with international research partners (Gallagher et al. 2013, 2020), in particular has explored the intersections of feminist theory (Gallagher 2016a), critical theory (Gallagher 2016c) and critical race theory (Gallagher & Rodricks 2017) within drama education practice and methodology (Gallagher 2006). Increasingly, this work aims to problematise earlier liberal framings of the 'civilising' value of arts education, drawing on international and multicultural perspectives (Rajendran 2014; Tam 2018; Tickle 2017; Villanueva & O'Sullivan 2020). Michael Finneran and Kelly Freebody's recent work has focused on mapping the interface between social justice and drama education (Finneran & Freebody 2016; Freebody & Finneran 2013, 2021), seeking to extend and problematise both the liberal and radical claims to social justice–focused practice in drama education via the theories of critical pedagogy. As they state, 'critical pedagogical and theoretical perspectives allow us a chance to provide a counter-narrative to the received idea that simply by intending to do "good", drama work will automatically always do "good"' (Finneran and Freebody 2016: 184). This social justice 'turn' within applied and educational drama and theatre scholarship is occurring in parallel to a similar social justice turn within Shakespearean scholarship (Eklund & Hyman 2019; Ruiter 2020a) and more broadly within public literary, theatrical and pedagogic Shakespeare engagement. This can be seen in the Shakespeare's Globe 'Shakespeare and Race' festival series and anti-racist workshops for teachers and young people, and in The Folger Shakespeare Library's Critical Race Conversations series 2020–1 (Folger Shakespeare Library 2021; Shakespeare's Globe Theatre 2020). Active Shakespeare pedagogy can, therefore, be said to inherit this critical genealogy from its parent disciplines of drama and theatre education *and* Shakespearean literary and performance scholarship.

Power

'Empowerment' is an oft-cited aim and claimed outcome of active Shakespeare approaches. Critical pedagogy is centrally concerned with the nature and relations of power, in particular the means by which current systems of power reproduce themselves, valorising some individuals, groups and sets of cultural practices and excluding others, and the means by which these power relations can be made visible, deconstructed and reconstituted along more equitable lines through education.

Power is not linear or singular but multidirectional and plural. As Michel Foucault has it: 'power is exercised from innumerable points, in the interplay of non-egalitarian and mobile relations' (Foucault, 1978: 94). Yet, in Foucault's examinations of the oppressive 'disciplinary' mode of power which he argues has become increasingly prevalent globally since the nineteenth century (Foucault 1975), there is a recognition of the insidious functions of dominant power structures. This disciplinary power framework is broadly in line with traditional critical pedagogy views on power, informed by Marxist and Freirean labour and class-based models which hold a clear, economic framework of power relations identifying the oppressed and the oppressor.

More networked models of power, such as critical geographer Doreen Massey's 'geometries of power' (Massey 2005), have been drawn on to explore and problematise the relationship between active participation and 'empowerment' within education (Gallagher 2008). These explorations re-frame empowerment not via the 'taking' or 'giving' of power, as if it were an object or resource, but instead see power as a 'diverse, ambivalent web of relations' (Gallagher 2008: 144) vital for public, social and civic life but everywhere weighted with imbalance. As Eklund and Hyman highlight, this model of social power is often leveraged within critical pedagogy literature because it offers a framework for thinking about power which not only allows us to identify and describe the ways it can be used to oppress and exclude but also allows for the recognition and creation of systems of power which function in more diverse, egalitarian ways, from multiple positions and perspectives. In their discussion of teaching Shakespeare for social justice, Eklund and Hyman emphasise that the core aim of critical pedagogy is to actively utilise theories of social power to facilitate change rather than merely offer critique: 'Even as we acknowledge that we are interpolated within a system, we own that it is interpolated within us. We must therefore recognize our responsibility not just to critique things as they are – potentially a sterile and self-serving practice – but also to transform them' (Eklund & Hyman 2019: 8–9)

This interdependent and networked 'web of power' model offers a useful grounding metaphor for navigating power in the active Shakespeare class-room in ways that facilitate substantive change. It can be useful to imagine, overlaid on our teaching spaces, the threads of power which both unite and bind us. We can question what broader systems these threads of power are holding up: which ones do we unthinkingly rely on, and which ones would we like to re-weave or attempt to sever altogether? What power relations do our students bring with them? Are these separate or different from ours? How can we weave these together more concretely, or tease them apart, to create a more diverse and balanced web?

Applied and educational drama scholars have frequently argued of the rich potential of the performative for not only making the 'webs of power' relations visible but also for actively de- and re-constructing them. For example, Viv Aitken's study of the 'spaces of participation' in applied theatre work demonstrates via Foucauldian and Freirean models of power how the explorative and imaginative practices of applied and educational theatre can facilitate an increase in agency for participants (Aitken 2009). Within this field of scholarship, analysis of educational power relations is often framed around spatial models, utilising theories of 'third space' (Bhabha 2004; Hulme et al. 2009; Soja 1999) to conceptualise the loosenings and reconfigurations of the 'power web' made possible via the use of drama and theatre-based pedagogies (Dolan 2006; Hunka 2015; Hunter 2008; Rodricks 2015; Sloan 2018). As Jonathan Heron and Nicholas Johnson emphasise, these conceptualisations focus on the sense of discovery, play and hope derived from the drama class/rehearsal room as a critical pedagogy 'laboratory' space, facilitating exploration and experimentation (Heron & Johnson 2017). Thomson and colleagues' large-scale empirical review of the UK arts education Creative Partnership programme demonstrated that these 'third spaces' created through arts education pedagogies can be potent but precarious (Thomson et al. 2012), emphasising their temporary, hybrid, permeable and flexible qualities. Active or drama-based pedagogy cannot easily claim to remove power relations in a liberatory act of transcendent social 'communitas' (Turner 1982), but it can offer opportunities to fruitfully play with its complex web. Liam Semler has explored this in an active Shakespeare education context via the concept of 'ardenspace' (Semler 2013).

Shakespeare has been seen as implicitly 'empowering' for young people and active Shakespeare as generating a liberating space to access this empowerment. Critical pedagogy offers a nuanced vocabulary of power to explore, refine and problematise these claims. As Neelands has emphasised, the 'uncrowning' of the teacher central to ensemble and active Shakespeare approaches is a socially risky, ongoing and negotiated process (Neelands & O'Hanlon 2011). Critical pedagogy invites us to pay forensic attention to how we enact this in practice through our teaching, rather than rely on it as a foregone conclusion of active work. Drama, by itself, does nothing (Freebody & Finneran 2021; Neelands 2004).

Conscientisation and Praxis

If power, with all its networked, oppressive and emancipatory potentiality, is the core concern of critical pedagogy, conscientisation and praxis are its core processes for seeking to act on and through power. Both terms originate with the work of Brazilian critical pedagogue Paulo Freire (1972, 2000). Conscientisation (*conscientização* in Freire's original) describes the process of becoming critically conscious of the social power relations both within and beyond the classroom. While praxis is the daily process of charting a lived relationship between social theory and educational practice: striving for a virtuous circle of practice-informed theorising and theory-informed practice. As Stephen Kemmis and Tracy Smith describe: 'praxis is what people do when they take into account all the circumstances and exigencies that confront them at a particular moment and then, taking the broadest view they can of what it is best to do, they act' (Kemmis & Smith 2008: 4). While both these terms could be said to fall under the accusation of critical pedagogy jargon, in the following, I hope to outline a clear definition of both and their relevance to active Shakespeare practice.

Both of these are rich and ongoing educational *processes*, a commitment, a perspective and a mode of thinking, teaching and being; not finite knowledge or a singular action. Teaching from a perspective of informed, critical curiosity is therefore one of the most valuable but demanding aspects of critical pedagogy work. Becoming 'woke', as in its original use by the US civil rights campaigners of the 1960s (Babulski 2020), is broadly synonymous to conscientisation, indicating – with a particular focus on racial power dynamics – the ongoing development of an awareness, a sense of reflective criticality on the broader forces, structures and institutions we are beholden to, and how they enact oppression on a variety of marginalised groups. Yet, recent western cultural discourses have sought to position critical educational and creative endeavours in fixed and binary terms, focusing on utilising the term 'woke' in a totalising, pejorative sense. Conservative cultural commentators have drawn on this reductive perspective in reference to more inclusive Shakespeare performance and casting practices (Cavendish 2020). This trend is further problematised by recent policy moves in the UK and the US contexts to remove critical race theory and related critical pedagogy approaches from use in educational contexts (Trilling 2020). This has had, in some cases, direct implications for teachers' choice of Shakespeare texts, with, for example, *The Tempest* being seen as engaging too directly in questions of race and colonialism (Espinosa 2019a). By highlighting the dynamic and processional nature of conscientisation, here, I emphasise the misplaced, prejudiced fear and denial which underpins these reductive responses to the rise of more critical perspectives within Shakespeare education and performance.

The concept of praxis reminds us that the use of critical social theory, including feminist, anti-racist and queer theories within educational contexts, is never finite or predetermined. As educators, we should neither fear these critical perspectives and practices nor treat them as a panacea. It is only how we actively engage with and embody them through daily and ongoing praxis that they have any concrete meaning within our teaching contexts. It is for this reason, as Shakespeare scholars have acknowledged (Dadabhoy & Mehdizadeh 2020), that active practices can so valuably act as an embodied touchstone for these processes – inviting conscious attendance to the interpersonal, civic and radical potential of our bodies in educational space (Thompson & Turchi 2020b).

Hope and Joy

The notion of hope runs deep through critical pedagogy theory and practice (Freire 2000). As Darren Webb describes it: 'The discourse of conscientisation is the discourse of transformative hope; a hope against the evidence that recognises the obstacles before it and yet grows in strength in spite of these' (Webb 2013: 410). There is a specificity and muscularity to the use of hope as an educational concept and practice within critical and social justice–focused pedagogy. Pragmatism scholar Judith Green would term this a social hope (Green 2008), recognising its *generative* quality – a commitment to a better world based not on generalised optimism but the dynamic and action-focused pragmatist concept of meliorism. Meliorism can be understood as 'the idea that at least there is a sufficient basis of goodness in life and its conditions so that by thought and earnest effort we may constantly make better things' (Nolan & Stitzlein 2011:3). Kathy

Hytten outlines the educational demands and opportunities of a meliorist social hope as a 'habit of the mind' for educators when she states 'It is a hope that compels us to act thoughtfully and creatively in the present so as to open up yet unimagined possibilities for the future – a hope that is generative, resourceful, engaged, and communal' (Hytten 2011: 1).

Hope is also frequently connected to joy within critical pedagogy. Freire states that 'There is a relationship between the joy essential to teaching activity and hope' (Freire 2000: 69) and argues for the radical democratising power of happiness and levity within the classroom (Freire 2016). As bell hooks acknowledges, there is a suspicion towards joy within the educational academy, a sense that educational practice led by joy is somehow lacking in rigour (hooks 2003). Yet, as feminist scholar Lynne Segal highlights, there is a longstanding critical and feminist recognition of the power of shared joy as the enactment of equitable and active citizenship (Segal 2017).

Given these dynamic, collaborative, affective and generative framings of joy and hope within critical pedagogy, it is perhaps to be expected that the concepts are frequently leveraged in applied and educational drama and theatre practice. In Neelands' ensemble pedagogy writings, he cites both Freire's considerations of critical hope and the then RSC Artistic Director Michael Boyd's discussion of hope in relation to his ensemble-based work with Shakespeare (Neelands 2009a). Boyd wrote in 2009 of his continuing hopes for his ensemble company, taking on a meliorist perspective when he states that hope will not in itself 'ensure success for our work, but [it does] describe the ambition behind our next risk' (Boyd 2009). In this, both Freire and Boyd speak of hope as 'essential' and 'descriptive' but as faciliatory of more specific goals, not an end itself, echoing the generative quality of collaborative and emancipatory work with Shakespeare in both performative and educational sectors.

Kathleen Gallagher, in her recent work exploring hope in theatre and drama education (Gallagher et al. 2020), echoes this critical, generative approach, emphasising in her analysis that social hope within drama education work is 'Not sentimental, saccharine fantasies of an unlikely future, but hopes grounded in present social relations, politically clear-eyed, critically and affectively engaged' (Gallagher 2015: 424). Freebody and Finneran have mapped the prominence of, and interrelations between hope, joy, criticality and drama (Freebody & Finneran 2021), while Winston has undertaken extended explorations of the educational and moral power of beauty, charm and laughter accessed within drama education practice (Winston 2008, 2010; Winston & Strand 2013). As I have emphasised throughout these first two sections, it is these deeply grounded pedagogic roots which inform active Shakespeare pedagogy, either obliquely or consciously.

In their book, *Teaching Shakespeare with Purpose*, Thompson and Turchi discuss the importance of hope to drive through 'the tyrannies' of teaching (Thompson & Turchi 2016: 11). This highlights the challenges which can be faced when employing a critically hopeful teaching practice in normative western educational contexts. Much critical pedagogy literature acknowledges this and seeks to remedy it through coping and solidarity strategies for teachers engaged in critical pedagogy work (Hytten 2011; Nolan & Stitzlein 2011). Yet, it has also been identified that within this critical pedagogy literature, practicing teachers are often seen as being in need of 'transformation' via critical pedagogy ideals (Pittard 2015). There is a parallel narrative present within drama education literature, in which the patchy or unrealised take-up of drama pedagogies within schools is framed as a deficit within teachers, a lack of hope or imagination (Araki-Metcalfe 2008; Stinson 2009). It is key here, therefore, to ground the generative, critically hopeful nature of active Shakespeare pedagogy and its potential for social justice, within the processional critical pedagogy practices of conscientisation and praxis. To teach with hope is a journey of discovery and development; to frame this either within a metricised deficit model or mythologised miracle model domesticates the richness, complexity and challenge of this journey.

This Element, therefore, functions as a piece of my own critical practice, in which I aim to articulate my own increasing conscientisation of the possibilities and problems of seeking social justice in the active teaching of Shakespeare. I do this with the hope that this articulation will prompt other scholars and teachers to similarly engage in their own ongoing conscientisation and seek to reflect on and develop their praxis in line with these discoveries. In the following three sections, I will expand on my understandings of active Shakespeare as a critical pedagogy endeavour via an outline of three overlapping areas of practice.

3 Playing as Reading the Text

As goes the oft-quoted statement from *Hamlet*: 'The play's the thing'. In Shakespeare education circles, this pithy phrase is often leveraged to emphasise the centrality of playfulness, enjoyment and fun within active approaches (Royal Shakespeare Company 2008; Winston 2013). This relies on the resonance between 'play' as a text for – and the action of – performance and 'play' as an idyllic childhood activity. See, for example, an opening statement of the RSC's 'Stand Up For Shakespeare' manifesto: 'Shakespeare wrote plays, and young children are geniuses at playing' (Royal Shakespeare Company 2008: 1). Joe Winston and Miles Tandy emphasise these resonances in their recommendations for exploring Shakespeare with primary and early years' students: 'It is no accident that we use the word *play* to describe both what happens when a child creates a cave [from a blanket and chairs] and what happens on the stage; and the subtle relationship between the two offers us rich opportunities to introduce the plays of Shakespeare' (Winston & Tandy 2012: 40). The creation of a 'playful ensemble' as central to its school festival project has been framed by the CSSF. In this, they leverage the notion of childhood play but also emphasise '[this] playfulness is different to the chaotic play of the playground: it is creative but structured and purposeful . . . it will empower your students to take risks during rehearsals; it will take the pressure off you by unlocking your students' creativity and encourage them to feel ownership of the play' (Shakespeare Schools Festival 2014). Senior Advisor of Creative Programmes at Shakespeare's Globe, Fiona Banks, similarly asserts the primacy of play when she describes the principles of Globe education practice as drawing from professional rehearsal processes of 'exploring the text actively, discovering aspects of the text by "playing". Playing their character but also being playful and experimental in their approach' (Banks 2014: 4). Thus, play within active Shakespeare is characterised as both developmentally natural and creatively purposeful.

In this section, I look beyond publicity copy and educational toolkit texts to explore the pedagogic principles behind these resonances between play, Shakespeare, performance and education. I argue this play-based approach is more substantial than generalised notions of fun and accessibility and offers an epistemological perspective on knowledge creation, which can be enacted at a variety of levels when engaging with Shakespeare texts through active approaches. I explore how this holds critical pedagogy implications both in terms of students developing autonomy with Shakespeare's complex texts and in terms of supporting an active and critical approach to knowledge production more broadly.

Play, Drama Education and Shakespeare

When early twentieth-century child psychologist Susan Issacs stated: 'Playing is the child's work', she provided a neat summary of the modern age's preoccupation with play and also its need to categorise and limit it in a clear binary with work and firmly in the realm of childhood. This highlights the obsession and also the suspicion that play holds in contemporary western society, and indeed many critics of active Shakespeare as an educational approach have derided this focus on play as evidence of its superficiality (McLuskie 2009; Wilson 1997).

Drama and theatre education research and practice has been much concerned with exploring the exact nature of these relationships between children's 'instinctive' developmental play and the creative play of performers and theatre professionals (Somers 2013), and with how to articulate the educational nature and potential of playful pedagogies. The history of this scholarship and reflective practice offers a nuanced reading of the critical potential of playful pedagogies. As discussed in Section 2, early twentieth-century drama education writers Harriet Finlay-Johnson and Henry Caldwell Cook both centred play in their writing on the value of drama-based pedagogy. Finlay-Johnson explores the capacity of play-focused teaching to create a 'natural' and humane education built on children's capacities and interests (Finlay-Johnson 1912), while Caldwell Cook was interested in the social and moral potential of bringing the civic values of 'fair play' into the classroom through collaborative and creative endeavours (Caldwell Cook 1917). This focus on play continued with the mid-twentieth-century drama education practitioner and writer Slade, who drew extensively on developmental models of children's play in framing his multi-stage theory of 'Child Drama' (Slade 1954). While these conceptualisations all function within the liberal 'civilising' model of the social value of drama in education, towards the end of the twentieth century and into the twenty-first century, drama and theatre education researchers and practitioners have continued to focus on the educational and social value of playfulness with a more radical and critical angle. Examples include Dunn's explorations of the power and autonomy young people draw from transgressive dramatic play (Dunn 2010), Neelands' argument for dramatic play as a 'proto-democratic' undertaking, in which young people learn to act equitably and collabora- tively in civic life as well as on the stage (Neelands 2016) and Winston's exploration of the social power of working fruitfully with the ambiguity and conflicting ideas which playful drama education facilitates (Winston 2005, 2013, 2015).

Through this brief mapping of drama and theatre education literature, we can firstly see how a focus on an explicitly playful pedagogy is grounded in the liberal aims of early and mid-twentieth-century progressive educa- tionalists, who understood children's play as an expression of authentic and engaged developmental experience (Dewey 1916; Piaget 1962; Vygotsky 1978). This section also explored how literature has increasingly engaged with the potential of play as a transgressive and critical educational process, facilitating reflective engagement, civic autonomy and social empower- ment. This focus on the critical, social potential of playfulness aligns with what play scholar Brian Sutton-Smith terms the 'second paradigm' of play research – as opposed to the psychological, developmental 'first paradigm' – in which play is conceived as a behaviour which is both in communication with and reflective of the larger society (Sutton-Smith 1979). Key examples of this second paradigm of play in research literature include anthropologist Victor Turner's study of socially transformative liminal rituals (Turner 1982) and cultural historian Johan Huizinga's considerations of humanity's contestive playing as the crucible of all cultural achievement (Huizinga 1949). Huizinga neatly summarises the second paradigm of play when he states civilisation 'arises in and as play and never leaves it' (Huizinga 1949: 12). Similarly, linguistic scholar Mikhail Bakhtin's theories of the socially transformative powers of the carnival (Bakhtin 1984) fall within the second paradigm of play, as do performance theorist Richard Schechner's writings on the revolutionary and personally empowering, if morally ambiguous, nature of dark and deep playfulness (Schechner 2012). In short, the playfulness of active Shakespeare can be best understood not as the simple developmental bridging of the binary between childhood play and the artistic discipline of theatrical play or as an engaging but frivolous prelude to the real 'work' of Shakespeare education but as a subjunctifying *mode* of action and interaction – common to children, performers and in fact humanity more broadly – which loosens behaviour from its everyday meanings and consequences (Bruner 1972) with all the rich potential for social reflection, resistance and re-imagining this implies.

Playing the Script

The educational scholar Margaret Mackey offers 'play' as an alternative verb to 'read' in educational contexts, suggesting it more accurately reflects the active, collaborative and intertextual processes which are undertaken by young people engaging with texts (Mackey 2004). This idea of 'playing the text' gives a flavour of the aims and tone of an active Shakespeare approach. It also highlights the critical pedagogy work inherent in playing as an interpretive act. For Mackey, the idea of 'playing' a text within a classroom is both a constructivist educational act ('The meaning of *play* as described is a medial one, it happens *between*' (Mackey 2004: 242)) and a progressive one ('Playing makes room for the agency and energy of performers [learners]' (Mackey 2004: 241)). In her study of 10–14 year-olds' literacy practices, Mackey charted how their collaborative, identity-led, multi-modal and intertextual 'playing' of their classroom texts facilitates engagement with confidence and fluency.

This interpretivist and constructivist understanding of reading as 'playing' the text frequently arises within active Shakespeare literature and resources. Winston, in highlighting the resonances between Bate's scholarship and the educational work of the RSC, argues it is through active playfulness that learners can 'tap into the twin energies of aspectuality and performativity' (Winston 2015: 30). Or as Stredder more succinctly phrases it: 'The point of . . . teaching methods using drama is to try to open up the texts as fields of play' (Stredder 2004: 6).

There are suggestions from some Shakespeare literary and cultural scholars (McLuskie 2009; Wilson 1997) that 'playing' Shakespeare is reductive and obscures the ability to engage in substantial and critical exploration of the texts: that you cannot both 'dance and think' with Shakespeare to use Kate McLuskie's metaphor. These arguments have been more substantively dealt with elsewhere, as in Tracy Irish's critique in which she draws on a range of neuroscience-informed performance and education research to emphasise how theatre-based educational practice can indeed 'embrace the complexities of the text by encouraging students to engage with the embodied nature of language as it communicates in action and in a moment' (Irish 2016: 14). I would push this further by highlighting not only the recent increased focus on playfulness within published Shakespearean scholarship (Gerzic & Norrie 2020) but also the range of playful and critical practices Shakespearean scholars frequently cite on social media. These include the creation of podcasts (NotAnotherShakespearePodcast 2020; thisshaxisgay 2020), the use and creation of memes in teaching and publications (Adams 2021) and jocular Facebook posts leading to scholarly writing (Barnden 2021). It is clear for these scholars that playing, or 'dancing', with Shakespeare absolutely informs their academic thinking and output. This dismissal and suspicion of the playfulness of active approaches can, therefore, be read as an act of 'domestication' in which the 'playing' is seen as an artificial pedagogical addition – a spoonful of sugar to wash down the perhaps initially unpalatable but ultimately beneficial medicine of Shakespeare. This view trivialises the critical, cultural and constructivist potential of playing the text in the ways explored in this section. Playing the text through active Shakespeare is not a precursor or obstruction to the 'real work' but the work itself. As Bate states: 'The meaning of a performance is to be found in the process of performance, which requires both writer and reader, actor and spectator … The working through does not *lead to a conclusion* it *performs the point*' (Bate 1997: 336, emphasis mine).

As Bate further discusses, Shakespeare's works are arguably particularly well suited to this playing of the text, due to Shakespeare's 'negative capability' to hold contradictory perspectives within his writing (Bate 1997: 330). The variety of the plays' source material, multiplicity of surviving editions and unrelenting frequency of historical and contemporary adaptations all speak to the continued capacity for playing with and through the texts (Taylor 1991). This interpretive multiplicity is grounded within the richness and ambiguity of the language itself and the complexity of its structure as a working text for performance. As Ruiter observes, there is also a temporal subjunctivity to many of the plays, giving examples such as Hal and Falstaff's repeated role-playing of the young prince's encounter with his father in *Henry IV* in which 'we see the reflected "was" and "is" as part of the formation of the future, the *could be*' (Ruiter 2020b: 8). As Neelands observes via Cornelius Castoriadis (Castoriadis 1997), this evidences the social imaginary potential within the texts: to reflect on the past, analyse the present and imagine possible futures through their consciously playful, performative frame (Neelands & O'Hanlon 2011).

Despite this richness and inherent performativity of the text itself, a sense of ambiguity is equally to be found in the gaps, silences and inconsistencies *surrounding* the text (Smith 2019a). This ambiguity and inconsistency are often framed as a rich moral positive, an indication of Shakespeare's commitment to a multifaceted humanity. But as others have highlighted, Shakespeare's texts – and our normative performances and framing of them – can also be deeply and unequivocally *in*humane, reproducing patriarchal, imperial and heteronormative discourses (Kemp 2019; Thompson 2011; Williams 2018). Playing the text is, therefore, a consciously critical act, seeking to unearth these both rich and troubling ambiguities and treat them with a clear-eyed consideration, as Thompson and Turchi argue: 'in a social justice framework, Shakespeare's homophobic, anti-Semitic, misogynistic and racist lines are not ignored, minimized, or laughed at. Instead, they are the starting point for interrogating complex texts, contexts and identities' (Thompson & Turchi 2020a: 55)

Coming back to Gibson's founding active Shakespeare principle of 'the plays as scripts', we can, therefore, understand 'playing' the text not as an additional gloss or introduction but the central interpretive act of the classroom. A primary educational purpose of using games and exercises from the realm of performance is to facilitate this dynamic, multifaceted reading of the texts. One of the clearest examples of this is the popular active exercise known as a 'Storywoosh' (Winston & Tandy 2012), which comprises a pacey, teacher-led storytelling of a Shakespeare play (or indeed any tale or literary text) where students, sat or stood in a circle, are invited into the centre to physicalise key moments and speak key lines of text.

The performance space is cleared periodically with a 'woosh' action and sound from the facilitator. While useful for quick exposition and engaging introductions to text, the core pedagogic quality of the 'woosh' is its playful nature. As Winston has emphasised: 'you cannot do it well and remain serious' (Winston 2008). It is the liberating, energising laughter that inevitably accompanies a good 'woosh', Winston argues, which facilitates a collaborative engagement with the text. While a 'woosh' alone does not offer much analytic or critical depth on a text, it is a clear example of how active Shakespeare approaches establish a shared, explorative 'playing' of the text from the outset.

In my study of schools' participation in CSSF's festival, I observed a variety of ways a deliberate playfulness with the text informed the educational and creative dimensions of the rehearsal process. Grace and her students, for example, at their inner London secondary school, frequently decentred normative or linear interpretations of the script throughout the rehearsal process with consciously playful approaches. These included the early creation of a mimed 'trailer', developed via explorative workshopping which prompted an embodied exploration of key themes and unfixing casting throughout rehearsals via small group scene explorations, ensuring character interpretation and dramaturgy remained a shared discursive process. Neelands and colleagues emphasise how the resultant learning from these playful processes is not just effective but reflective and critical: 'The "doing" is continuously interrupted for reflection' (Monk et al. 2011b: 69).

Playing the Word and the World

In practicing and researching active Shakespeare teaching approaches, I have often found it useful to differentiate the level of focus on which this interpretive playing is operating – are we playing the *word* or the *world* of the text? By this, I mean either exploring the text at the level of language, form and structure (playing the word) or at the level of character, story and theme (playing the world). This helps to draw out the critical implications of 'playing the text' into an engaged praxis in which the teacher or facilitator can more consciously consider the mode, nature and purpose of the text playing taking place.

Language- and voice-focused approaches, such as those developed by RSC voice practitioner Cicely Berry (Berry 2004, 2008), are central to 'playing the word' practices of active Shakespeare pedagogy. Berry's techniques seek to move beyond intellectual readings of Shakespeare's text and language and, as Winston describes it, 'connect with the sounds, the rhythms, the music of Shakespeare's language at a very deep level of feeling' (Winston 2015: 38). Berry's approach to voice and language work, in addition to providing an embodied methodology for technical, close-text analysis, also offers one way to circumnavigate issues of uncritical reproduction of elitist cultural values through Shakespeare education. Highlighting the immediacy, this musical and embodied approach can foster, she argues: 'because Shakespeare's writing is our literary heritage, we too often feel we have to honour its literary status, thus forgetting . . . all the heat in the language, the coarseness, the violence, the passion, the sorrow . . . I so often feel we have lost its roughness, and therefore we lose the immediacy of its impact – its basic reality' (Berry 2008: 6)

The possibilities of this are suggested in Winston's study of an Early Years' RSC education project, in which he draws on ideas of language play from linguist Guy Cook (2000) to analyse how the project opened up opportunities for participants to play through and with the rich and ambiguous language (Winston 2013). Echoing Berry's approach, Cook posits that young children engage in playful language learning through *form* as readily as with *meaning*, indicating the critical educational impact of an approach to playing the word grounded in experience, rather than narrowly focused on developing comprehension. An example of this form of playing in action could be seen in one of my CSSF case study schools: in an opening workshop with her year 5 (age 9–10) students, the majority of whom have EAL, primary teacher Rachel encourages her class during a whole group language exercise to 'Murmur the words in your mouth, like it's a really delicious sweet'. This session was the first introduction to the language of their play, and Rachel focused on this experiential, explorative approach. No attempt was made at defining particular words or checking students' comprehension of the text: the aim was an explorative, embodied and aesthetic experience.

Playing the word approaches can be found in a variety of critical and social justice–focused Shakespeare teacher practices including, for example,

Noor Desai's use of close text 'riffing'. 'Close reading begins ... with riffing' he explains to his undergraduate students: 'it does not see the plays as storehouses of hidden meanings; it sees them as a musical key within which we are encouraged to improvise' (Desai 2019: 32). This worked in practice via regular student assignments to select a single word or event from the text, map all associations this word or event held for the student and use this as a basis for more extended analysis and critique. Desai reflects on how this not only opened up novel interpretations of the Shakespeare texts in question but also helped to 'topple the walls that privilege Shakespeare's face over students' lives' (Desai 2019: 34). Carla Della Gatta similarly argues how explorative close language work with Shakespeare can function as critical, social justice–focused pedagogy through its invocation to critically explore the relationship between language and power. In her Shakespeare teaching practice, Della Gatta seeks to connect explorative close-text work with developing in her students the empowered criticality needed to navigate the twenty-first-century public discourse of 'fake news' and 'alternative facts' (Della Gatta 2019). Playing the word through active Shakespeare practice, whether in the early years, primary school or undergraduate classroom, is much more than 'technical' close language work. It offers a micro word-by-word framework for destabilising the complex power webs woven around and through Shakespeare's rich, ambiguous and historical texts by facilitating an embodied exploration with the language as the point of entry.

Playing the world, by contrast, can be understood as interpretive playing with a macro lens, exemplified by the pro-social and citizenship approaches of Jonothan Neelands (Monk et al. 2011b; Neelands 2010b; Neelands & O'Hanlon 2011). This playing draws on both professional rehearsal practices (Winston 2015) and the experiential traditions of process drama and theatre-in-education. Both of these influences are visible in a short video of Neelands' teaching practice in a primary school setting, in which teacher-in-role work is used deftly to give a performative and explorative framing to the experiences of Cordelia in the opening scenes of *King Lear* (Neelands 2008). Within active Shakespeare literature, 'playing the world' is typically referred to as exploring themes, characters and story within the texts, and, unfortunately, it is in discussions of this area of work where the toolkits tend to revert to universalised expressions of Shakespeare's relevance, as discussed in Section 1. For example, when Banks states the plays 'are universal stories . . . The stories are timeless and enable students to gain perspective, a sense of themselves and of the universality of the human condition' (Banks 2014: 10). As I will explore in more detail in the following section, this assumption of universal themes forecloses opportunities for students both to find specific resonances based on their own knowledges and to fully critique problematic elements of the texts.

It is perhaps for this reason that literary scholars and active teachers of Shakespeare alike are at times sceptical about the opportunities for criticality and analytic depth in broader 'playing the world' practices, particularly where they see this as entailing a simplified 'translation' of original text to 'modern' language through role-play exercises (Blank 2014; Thompson & Turchi 2016). Stredder talks of the challenges of utilising role-play and improvisation with Shakespearean characters and stories in teaching, suggesting that without a sufficiently focused critical and textual frame these can simply *replace* the ideas of the text with students' existing knowledges and perspectives, rather than facilitate an active encounter between the two (Stredder 2004: 191–2). But, while playing the world should be focused and specific in order to be meaningful, this does not mean it has to be 'small' or stay close to the text in its framing and approach. For example, Nora William's practice-based work *Measure (Still) for Measure* invites young people to undertake holistic re-imaginings of *Measure for Measure* grounded in a feminist critique of the text's gender politics (Williams 2018). The outcomes of these re-imaginings vary from group to group but typically undertake bold reworkings of the text informed by 'non-hierarchical, practical, and collaborative' approaches to editing and storytelling. Many other social justice–focused Shakespeare educators have found pairing texts with alternative source material a fruitful way to frame deep and critical playing of Shakespeare's worlds; a practice discussed in literature and language arts social media platforms via the hashtag #DisruptTexts. This can be seen in Desai's contrast of Othello's final monologue with Audre Lorde's poems '1978' and 'Power' (Desai 2019) or Hobgood's use of irreverent film, manga and chatroom-based adaptations of *Macbeth* to interrogate the portrayal of madness and disability within the play (Hobgood 2019). Playing the world of the Shakespeare text through these judicious pairings invites specific critical textual analysis within a creative and multi-modal pedagogy.

As Hatfull and Mookherjee demonstrate in their recent exploration of adaptation as 'fracking' Shakespeare (Hatfull & Mookherjee 2021) 'playing' the words and worlds of Shakespeare can be as critical and anarchic with the language, character and story as it can be appreciative or gently curious. Similarly drama education scholars have explored how 'dark' (Schechner 2012), deep and risky play can hold equal cultural and educational value alongside the light-hearted playfulness typically recognised in educational settings (O'Toole 2001; Winston 2005). Revisiting the core critical pedagogy principle of social constructivism, I argue that these consciously active, explorative and playful approaches to Shakespearean texts support a relationship with the playtexts for the learner of productive intimacy rather than distanced admiration. Playing the text, as advocated in active Shakespeare literature and practice, is not merely an accessible introduction or preamble; it frames a variety of analytic approaches to the language and themes of the plays. This holds critical pedagogy implications in terms of students charting an autonomous and engaged relationship with Shakespeare's complex written texts and global cultural significance. In Section 4, I turn to the parallel consideration of how, alongside fruitfully deconstructing and destabilising the Shakespearean text, the active Shakespeare classroom can facilitate a valuing and centring of learners' existing knowledges, identities and positionalities.

4 Identity and Care in the Active Shakespeare Classroom

If exploratively playing the text is one side of the constructivist coin of critical active Shakespeare, then a care-led approach which foregrounds students' existing knowledge and identities is the other. Playing the text, as explored in the previous section, can be seen as fruitfully 'destabilising' and opening up Shakespeare for active and contextualised interpretation. The play of active Shakespeare does more than simply leave space for learners. It establishes a mutual rapport, a lived experience of collaboration, a greater sense of intimacy with each other as well as the text which is vital to foregrounding students' positionalities and knowledges.

In this section, I therefore explore a feminist critical pedagogy focus on identity, community and care in relation to active Shakespeare practice. I highlight the ways in which active Shakespeare approaches foreground such identity work within the classroom by valuing and drawing on on learners' existing knowledge and holistic identities. I also examine how the collaborative learning framework of active Shakespeare supports the development of civic care, a core principle within feminist critical pedagogies. I connect these techniques with broader applied and educational drama and theatre pedagogy concepts such as communitas and ensemble. Furthermore, I draw on feminist, critical and post-colonial theatre and drama education research to demonstrate the social justice potential of such pedagogic approaches. To explore the enactment and implications of these approaches in practice, I compare two case studies from my research with CSSF, analysing how the relative enactments of identity, community and care-led pedagogy affected the rehearsal process and the project outcomes for both groups.

Care- and Identity-Led Pedagogy in Drama and Theatre Education

'The personal is political' has long been a feminist mantra. It is in the vein of this statement that feminist critical pedagogy literature has often focused on the radical and emancipatory potential of education practices grounded in full and complex expressions of teachers' and learners' identities (Baxter 2002, 2015; Grady 2003; Rohrer 2018; Sharkey 2004) and interpersonal acts of care, love and joy (Baines 2013; Gallagher 2016a; Henry 1992; Hughes 2019; Noddings 2013; Segal 2017; Tronto 2017; Vincent 2016). Within this body of literature and practice, care- and identity-led pedagogies are positioned as central to social justice because they both celebrate and substantively draw on the diverse knowledges, perspectives and identities in the room (Rohrer 2018; Yosso 2005) and because they model empathetic and emancipatory civic practices (Kitchen 2021; Sloan 2018).

Freebody and Finneran deftly summarise how identity and care are frequently indicated within drama in education scholarship, where there is a recurring idea of practice and performance-based work as literally and figuratively 'giving a voice' to young people and participatory group work as similarly facilitating a sense of agency and community (Freebody & Finneran 2021). They also, however, highlight the importance of problematising this, rather than making simple or mythologised assumptions about any inherent 'power' dramatic and active approaches might hold to achieve these ends (Freebody & Finneran 2021: 19–20). Moving beyond these generalised claims was a focus of Gallagher and colleagues' most recent multi-site drama education study, in which they sought at each international site to explore the relationship between interpersonal and civic caring within drama and how this is understood and enacted in different social and geographic contexts (Gallagher 2015). As Myrto Pigkou-Repousi, the Greek site project leader, argues, the study revealed how a care-led pedagogy embraces students' experiences and concerns as the foundation for learning via the affordances of performative practice (Pigkou-Repousi 2020). Winston and colleagues have further theorised these practices as being defined by a commitment to dialogic civic exchange and outlined how the performative, explorative and 'subjunctive' nature of drama and theatre education practice facilitates this (Winston 2005; Winston & Strand 2013).

This care- and student identity–led focus within drama education practice has been studied and conceptualised via a variety of 'space-making' theories. This can be seen in Bethany Nelson's exploration of youth community-building through devised theatre practices (Nelson 2011b, 2011a), Cathy Sloan's analysis of the potential of applied theatre practice with adults with substance misuse to co-create 'live' affective spaces in which change is possible (Sloan 2018), Rachel Turner-King's focus on the practice of welcoming young people's holistic identities within community youth theatre spaces (Turner-King 2018), Charlene Rajendran's exploration of the 'post-colonial conviviality' possible within multicultural youth theatre work in Singapore (Rajendran 2014, 2016) and Gallagher's exploration of the drama education classroom enacted as 'family', which explicitly focuses on the critical race- and feminist-informed emancipatory potential of 'othermothering' (Henry 1992; Hughes 2019) within education (Gallagher 2016a). These overlapping analyses of the drama education space as convivial, community-led, familial and affective represent a converging set of discursive and socio-cultural theory-informed expressions of the complex but often ephemeral experience of the collaborative drama education classroom and its potential to further critical social justice aims. These conceptualisations of educational spaces and how they are constructed and navigated speak back through ecological models of cultural power (Massey 2005) to questions of how active Shakespeare practice can destabilise monolithic power structures around Shakespeare in the classroom and facilitate a more polyphonic, equitable approach.

Care and Identity in Active Shakespeare Literature and Practice

In the studies cited earlier, the focus is often on devised and improvised drama forms, such as verbatim theatre, oral history performance and collective devising (Gallagher et al. 2020). Yet, this work is developed from the same drama and theatre education principles as active Shakespeare practice, and the same bedrock of identity-led care underpins the work here also. As literary scholar Peter Thomson expresses it: 'Shakespeare was not writing plays for posterity, but texts for performance by people he knew well. He relied on their competence, composed towards their capacity' (Thomson 2002: 140). The rich and purposefully 'gappy' (Smith 2019a) nature of Shakespeare's texts can, therefore, be read not only as an invitation to bring the reader or performer's whole self but also as an assurance that Shakespeare quite literally wrote space for his performers into the texts. Active and critical approaches to teaching Shakespeare, therefore, align with a sense of mutual civic care and engagement and a locally contextualised, identity-led approach to the text.

Recent literature exploring inclusive and social justice–focused approaches to teaching Shakespeare has highlighted the central role active approaches can play in supporting student identity–led ways into the texts (Eklund & Hyman 2019; Homan 2019b; O'Dair & Francisco 2019). See, for example, Rochelle Smith's discussion of the social gains of the Shakespeare performance festival she hosts for her remote Maryland students in the Appalachian mountains (Smith 2019b), or Ruben Espinosa's exploration of the relationship between Chicanx and Lantinx communities and Shakespeare charted through performance (Espinosa 2019a). The pedagogic quality of these identity-led encounters with Shakespeare can be summarised by Naomi Conn Liebler's description of how her students' existing knowledges and perspectives have become central to her teaching: 'Increasingly, I find I am not so much "delivering" Shakespeare to my heterogeneous and ethically/racially diverse student population as I am tapping into what they already know, experientially, in order to clear a path for them to forge their own connections' (Conn Liebler 2019: 179).

A similar perspective can be seen expressed in the RSC's active Shakespeare toolkit, with the emphasis that the resource aims to offer 'opportunities for pupils to discover new things about a play with their whole selves: bodies, hearts and minds' (Royal Shakespeare Company 2010: 9). Likewise, as discussed in Section 1, Gibson highlights students' existing cultural knowledges as central in interpretations of the text when he states 'All students should have opportunities through practical experience to make up their own minds about what Shakespeare might hold for them' (Gibson 2016: 7) or when he emphasises 'crucial resources are the teacher's own attitudes, knowledge and capacities, and the particular circumstances of the school or college' (2016: 21). Stredder, similarly, discussed active approach's

> philosophical foundations in student-centred and progressive thinking, [which] may also mean that the 'active classroom' is a particularly receptive and responsive environment. By valuing and harnessing positive social connections and fore-grounding participatory procedures it has available, I would argue, a broader, richer and more versatile means of supporting students, whatever their needs and abilities, than is normally found in traditional class-rooms.
> (Stredder 2004: 129–30)

However, this progressive and humanist focus on student and teacher identities is not always fully realised in the more directly practice-focused, exercise repository sections of the active Shakespeare literature. A nuanced example of this can be found though further analysis of Stredder's discussions of student identity in *The North Face of Shakespeare*. Notably, Stredder recognises the development of critical social theory surrounding identity and discusses its implications for character analysis when he states: 'We are perceived to behave as subjects of the discourses of power, of class, race, culture and religion and must live, in part, in the way these discourses define us' (Stredder 2004: 82). Stredder also emphasises that active Shakespeare teachers should, on this basis, take account of critical social theory in character analysis and highlights a sense of synergy between active and critical approaches here, emphasising: 'practical approaches seem to mirror the diversity of contemporary critical theory and to resist the monolithic and universal' (2004: 82–3). Furthermore, he specifically *does* go on to suggest student casting will have a core impact on this: 'In the drama workshop, versions of the characters proliferate and diversify, springing out in all directions, even as the actors speak, interact and invent the action' (2004: 83). Yet, crucially, the language Stredder uses to describe this proliferation realised through students' embodiment of character is markedly different to his discussion of the critical social context of Shakespeare's *characters*: 'The suggestions of active work are based on the notion of workshop participants inhabiting and exploring particular roles, using all their own personal skills and abilities (in thought, feeling, imagination, movement, expression) to take up and animate those roles. Students with different voices, shapes, styles, gestures and idiosyncrasies, become new expressions, in body and presence, of characters' (2004: 91)

Characters are considered in terms of the intersectional and socialised identities, such as 'class, race, culture and religion', whereas *learners'* identities are by contrast notably de-politicised, relying on aesthetic and humanistic notions of 'voices, shapes, styles, gestures and idiosyncrasies'. This avoids a consideration of how these individual elements might be constitutive of more socially positioned identities. In this framing, a direct and deeper consideration of the interface between learners' and characters' identities is, therefore, frustratingly missed. The rationale for this desaturated language around learner identity is indicated in Stredder's separate discussion of identity and 'difference' in regard to ensemble and group formation exercises: 'Differences in gender, culture, ethnicity, sexual orientation and belief are obviously fundamental to people's sense of themselves, and for all the drive towards cohesion that practical work entails, it is well never to forget these personal differences, many of which may be 'hot' – areas of great sensitivity for individuals' (2004: 145)

There is a further implication that such 'hot' differences should not be addressed directly in the active Shakespeare classroom when Stredder goes on to explain: 'Sometimes, where differences are relatively 'cool' and uncontroversial, we can acknowledge and work with them directly' (2004: 145). While this is a valuable recognition that students' experiences and expressions of identity can be highly personally and culturally charged and are not simply resources for teachers to utilise, there is also a concerning implication here of *which* student 'differences' or issues are considered too 'hot' for the active Shakespeare classroom. Compare this perspective, for example, with the effective banning of *The Tempest* in one Arizona school for fear 'that teaching *The Tempest* would inevitably lead students, on their own, to recognize "the themes [of race and oppression] and decide to write, discuss or ask questions in class," (Biggers 2012) which would be in direct violation of the law' (Espinosa 2019b: 77). While Stredder's observations and recommendations undoubtedly come from both a place of care for students and teachers as well as an appreciation of the power and 'heat' of identity work developed over his long teaching career, the conclusion to simply avoid such 'hot differences' is concerning, holding troubling implications for *which students'* identities and experiences may therefore be considered 'unworkable', that is, those which include marginalised genders, sexualities, cultures and ethnicities.

Likewise, Gibson does little within *Teaching Shakespeare* to directly connect the progressive educational principles outlined within the book's opening to the specifics of the exercises offered in the practice-based 'toolkit' sections. For example, within the book, Shakespeare is credited with 'granting' or 'unlocking' (2016: 4–7): 'self-awareness', 'confidence', 'self-esteem', 'empathy' and engagement in 'moral issues' (2016: 6). This perspective, in which students are 'granted' a deeper or more nuanced identity via engagement with Shakespeare, is not unique to active Shakespeare literature. See, for example, Australian high schoolteacher Sarah Golsby-Smith's analysis of how her apparently 'sullen', 'shy', 'garrulous' and 'awkward' adolescent students, via a drama-based encounter with Shakespeare, discover a '"self" that they *did not know they had*'

(Golsby-Smith 2013: 127, emphasis mine). While citing the variety of imaginative interpretations her students developed in response to their studied text, ultimately Golsby-Smith celebrates their 'understanding' and 'comprehension' (2013: 132) of the text and how the performance-based education encountered with it brought the students into creation as individuals, from a sullen adolescent mass to confident, literally upstanding individuals ('their posture began to change. Shoulders back, heads up'; 2013: 131). In this encounter, 'Shakespeare' – the text and the cultural icon – remains unchanged, though better understood and appreciated, and the students are positioned as underformed, in need of transformation and 'creation'. The difference between the Shakespeare classroom, being a site for *expressing* and *utilising* a greater range of learners' existing knowledge and identity positionalities, and a site where identities are actually *created* through the power of the encounter with Shakespeare is nuanced but paramount. There is a need here to be meticulous about the power ecologies implicit in such statements and who or what is granted agency through them. Was the new level of expression and engagement that Golsby-Smith describes actually *created* through dramatic encounter with Shakespeare or did the students rather feel empowered and valued to *express* a greater individuality in the collaborative drama processes, compared to the pedagogies of normative western school system which so often values conformity and narrow academic achievement?

Stredder's engagement with identity within the active Shakespeare classroom demonstrates both the rich possibilities and inhibiting concerns surrounding the power and potential of privileging student identities, experiences and knowledges in an active analysis of Shakespeare's texts. Yet, without specific and sustained consideration of the social and cultural implication of this engagement within active Shakespeare literature, it is too easy to slip from this rich potential to reductive and deficit notions of marginalised learners as in need of 'transformation' and Shakespeare as holding an inherent cultural power to achieve this. For all the initially uplifting implications of such 'transformations', we must ask the following two questions: (1) What discourses of power and autonomy are being reinforced in these narratives? (2) What specificities of identity and experience are being obscured? As Thompson and Turchi state: 'We think it is important to interrogate the purpose and value of being blind to identity differences in the Shakespeare classroom. Who benefits from a race-free, gender-free, sexuality-free and ability-free approach? ... there is no better place to talk about complex identity issues than in a classroom that engages Shakespeare's complex texts' (Thompson & Turchi 2016: 13)

Clearly, as Ambereen Dadabhoy and Nedda Mehdizadeh have argued, there is a need for greater intercultural communication and racial literacy training (Dadabhoy & Mehdizadeh 2020) in order to support confident, empathetic and more sustained engagement with issues of identity perceived as potentially too 'hot' to handle if the social justice potential to explore our complex identities through Shakespeare's complex texts is to be realised. Thompson and Turchi suggest one way forward here via the use of conscious 'casting' practices in the classroom (Thompson & Turchi 2020a: 56–7). While this has valuable implications in focusing teachers' considerations of performance as centrally grounded in the physical and social aspectuality of our bodies, I would suggest what is missed in this is an acknowledgement of the history of representational performance in social justice–oriented theatre and drama education. See, for example, the work of non-naturalistic dramaturgs such as Brecht and explorative representational practices such as Boal's Image and Forum theatre (Gallagher & Jacobson 2018; Neelands 2010c). Active Shakespeare practices draw on these representational and non-naturalistic traditions, for example, the use of character 'archetypes' within Shakespeare Globe Education practice (Banks 2014: 38) or more generally the use of rehearsal room games and exercises, which actively explore characters, themes and plots without necessarily 'casting' scenes in the theatrical sense, as seen in Stredder's 'soliloquy machine' exercise (Stredder 2004: 158–9). Recent active Shakespeare research (Cheng & Winston 2011), including my own as I discuss in more detail in the following, is more directly exploring the reflexive relationality of a care- and identity-led route through active Shakespeare practice both within specific in-role work and within the foundational 'ensemble' principles of active practice.

Identity Work in Active Shakespeare Practice

As drama education scholar Pru Wales argues, the embodied, co-constructed nature of drama and theatre-based teaching invites a reflexive and critical focus on teacher identity and positionality in the classroom: 'It is only in gaining an understanding of how the personal social and political can enter the drama teachers' classrooms and are applied to teaching practices that they can begin to comprehend how their work can simultaneously educate and inhibit, free and constrict their students' (Wales 2009: 261)

Within my case study research into schools' participation in CSSF's festival project, a key strand of analysis focused on the participating teachers' identity work in the classroom: how and to what extent this modelled and invited a valuing of students' identities and existing knowledges. Here, I compare the practices of two teachers: firstly, Grace, the teacher in the core case study; secondly, Travis, a teacher in one of the preceding pilot studies. Both teachers ran the CSSF festival project on consecutive years at the same school, an inclusive secondary school in inner London. Both worked with their respective GCSE drama class groups – nine students in Grace's case and fourteen in Travis', aged between 14 and 16. Both groups reflected the diverse, working-class demographic of the local area, with a mix of South Asian British, Black British, White British, White European and mixed-race students in each class. I focus first on the ways in which Grace's holistic identity-led teaching and classroom practice modelled and invited a corresponding holistic expression of her students' diverse identities and knowledges. I then turn to Travis' teaching practice and how his narrower and metricised framing of both his own and his students' identities inhibited the creative and collaborative work of their performance project.

Entering and leaving Grace's classroom was 'bracketed' by periods of social and playful interaction where the cast and director oriented and grounded themselves as a group in readiness for the rehearsal process: within the games and jokes, issues of school, community and interpersonal conflict were attended to, as were practices of religious devotion when Ramadan coincided with the rehearsals. Over time, the games and banter of these brackets folded in ongoing shared jokes and a selected 'theme song'. Notably, while these brackets were spaces for the cast to express and explore each other's identities, they were also increasingly a space in which their Shakespeare text informed those jokes and interactions, as one student reflected during a focus group: 'All our quotes are . . . Shakespeare quotes!' (27 November 2014).

Grace did not rush or minimise these nominally 'off task' periods but participated in them fully without formalising them or imposing a structure.

These brackets can be understood as a social ritual, analogous to Turner's notion of liminality (Turner 1982). As I have discussed in more detail elsewhere (Kitchen 2021, 2022), the care-led and culturally responsive educational practices extended through these brackets created a sense of 'family' within the cast:

Saguna: It's like a family, (laughs) it really is. (Focus Group, 27 November 2014)

Jocelyn: Yeah, I was thinking like, we're treated like family. (Focus Group, 27 November 2014)

Grace: That's been a godsend really, I think the process of doing it as a mixed year group, um, group of young people has brought them together, they're a little community ... they're a little family. (Teacher interview, 27 November 2014)

Grace's holistic and care-led pedagogy developed this sense of family, often in ways grounded in her identity as a new mother and her genuine engagement in her students' family lives; for example, inquiring after student Jocelyn's expectant mother and offering to pass on baby clothes. Likewise, Grace regularly spoke of her restless nights with her son and logistical challenges of childcare. The students half-jokingly offered to babysit, and Grace's childcare arrangements were part of the shared planning of theatre trips for CSSF training and performance days. Her mothering and caring, both of her own child and the students as 'children' of the classroom 'family', were thus central to the CSSF project.

The pedagogy of 'mothering' can be read as a counter-hegemonic enactment of civic care within the classroom which can be undertaken by teachers of any gender, regardless of their actual parenting status. There is a history within feminist and critical race pedagogy of exploring the educational work of 'othermothers' (Gallagher 2015; Henry 1992): female educators, traditionally of Afro-Caribbean origin, who work within a 'cultural tradition of mothering other people's children as an emancipatory practice' (Gallagher 2016a). Within this case study, Grace's construction of her role as a teacher through her personal and local identities can be read as a feminist resistance to the institutional models of school care and control (Gallagher 2016a; Noddings 2013; Tronto 2017; Yosso 2005). This, in turn, activates the pedagogic potential of students' 'familial capital' – the extended models of community, family and caring – which urban student populations and students of colour frequently bring to the classroom (Nelson 2011b; Sennett 2012; Yosso 2005). This familial capital was then drawn on throughout the rehearsal process, both in the interpretation and performance of the Shakespeare text, as I explore further in Section 5, as well as in the navigation of interpersonal conflict within and beyond the class and in a more equitable approach to institutional requirements, as I have explored elsewhere (Kitchen 2021, 2022).

In focus group sessions, the students reflected on the value they found in this experience of co-creating and participating in a playful Shakespeare ensemble 'family':

Arthur: Yeah, I'd agree with that everyone has their own special way of doing something and, it kind of shows other people that 'Oh, that looks good I can try that myself' and then everyone's sharing their ideas so –

Eleanor: Yeah.

Arthur: – it's making everything better.
　　　　. . .

Tapani: Yeah, I think you can be more in, yourself in drama than in other lessons because, like, I dunno, you're more, open to do more stuff and its practical stuff . . .

Arthur: Yeah, yeah. Me, I kind of see myself as a kind of weird person, and in drama I can kind of use that weirdness to kind of create a character a bit and make the character a bit more effective. And give it more personality.

(Focus Group, 17 July 2014)

Here, students Arthur and Tapani reference the inclusive and collaborative nature of their classroom ('everyone's sharing their ideas'), and the active ('its practical stuff') and performative ('to . . . create a character') context, demonstrating how within active Shakespeare work, a care-led pedagogy can combine with 'playing' the text to centre students' existing knowledges and identities ('I . . . see myself as kind of a weird person').

Travis, the previous year's CSSF festival project leader, took a very different approach to identity work within the CSSF classroom. During interviews, drama teacher Travis repeatedly grounds his definition of his teaching identity in terms of the metrics of the mainstream UK school system. He emphasises his own teaching qualifications as an 'advanced skills teacher' and states: 'Every observation I've had I've always been outstanding' (Interview 2, 27 November 2013). As Mary Klein has argued, teachers are not always able to position themselves with reflexivity and agency if they are overly 'caught up' in previously successful professional discourses (Klein 1998). Travis similarly framed his students' identities within these same metricised frameworks, in an interview discussing the CSSF cast as: 'very, very weak' academically. In this, he focused on their additional learning needs; and their being 'pathway three students' in the school's lexicon, that is, 'they have three years and six hours a week to obtain a C at GCSE [English], due to the fact they came in well below national average on literacy at key stage two' (Interview 2, 27 November 2013). What is telling about these descriptions, as with Travis' own narrative of his school identity, is that they largely draw on the metric-driven discourses of normative schooling: labelling students as inherently deficient and expressing their achievement in the numerical or finite grades of high-stakes testing. This deficit framing extended to discussions of the students' cultural identities, as when Travis states he sees the value of CSSF as:

> Them on stage, overcoming the fear of something that potentially is very alien to them, especially you know, in socially deprived areas . . . So you've not only got your, low aspirations, your low literacy but one of the big deficiencies you've got in inner-city areas is a cultural gap, a significant culture gap . . . they, they never go to the theatre, ever. They never experience any museums, *any form of cultural experiences* and I think something like this, well, just goes a step towards bridging that culture gap.
> (Interview 1, 16 July 2013, emphasis mine)

This 'redemptive' model of Shakespeare bridging disadvantaged students' 'culture gap' is thoroughly critiqued in Barnes' nuanced analysis of film documentaries depicting marginalised youths' encounters with Shakespeare (Barnes 2020). Barnes discusses how this narrative of 'redemptive' Shakespeare married with assumptions of marginalised youths' educationally and culturally deficient identity aligns with the 'new paternalism' movement in schooling. His book explores how the 'tough love' and 'no excuses' mantras of this movement stems not only from a pedagogic intention to replace the culture of 'the streets' with one of hegemonic 'excellence' (Barnes 2020: 50) but also from a much deeper cultural policy rhetoric which distrusts and is threatened by the various non-nuclear, non-patrilineal models of many non-western family and community constructs. In the new paternalism model of schooling: 'the figure of the father [is] one whose mental hygiene will wash away pathology, . . . one whose discipline will modify the behaviour of those unwilling to delay gratification, whose paternity will, through the discourses of self-help, transform and bring into the fold of middle-class respectability those historically excluded' (Barnes 2020: 56)

Travis' paternalistic active Shakespeare identity work, and the educational and cultural rhetorics it evokes, can be contrasted with Grace's 'othermothering' teacher identity. New paternalism forecloses opportunities for student-led engagement both with each other and the Shakespeare text while 'othermothering' extends them. As Ayanna Thompson argues, within the redemptive and transformational rhetorics of new paternalism: 'Shakespeare symbolically stands in for a body politic that seeks both to accept and to digest/melt away the racial, ethnic, cultural and social differences' (Thompson 2011: 130). This approach, of nominally seeking relevance within Shakespeare for diverse and marginalised students but ultimately framing this within a deficit assumption of their cultural identity, could be seen in Travis' decision, before beginning to work with the cast, to direct a 'gritty, working-class' production of their play, *Macbeth*. However, as his students reflected in their focus groups, this decision did not resonate with them:

Craig: He said talk cockney and that yeah, but he's not really . . . he ain't told us to actually *do* it because sometimes . . . Like he's saying talk cockney but . . .

James: [indistinguishable] stereotypes actually, because he was like 'you'll
      know it well because of the area that you're from'.

Craig: . . . And sometimes he takes the mick, like before we was listening to
      music and he was like 'turn that *hood* music off' or something.

Jack: And then he wants us, and then he wants us *to do it for him* and that.
                       (Focus Group, 1 October 2013, emphasis mine)

Here, the students identify Travis' reading of their identity and community
as an act of 'stereotyping'. They report confusion and frustration with the
invitations to 'talk cockney' and draw on their own (assumed) cultural
identity. Specifically, they are describing an experience of being asked to
perform a preconceived notion of 'urban' ('he wants us to do it for him')
both without an acknowledgement of how 'urban' identities are normally
minimised within the school (i.e. 'turn that hood music off') or the space to
discover resonances between the Shakespeare text and their experiences on
their own terms. In this case, this sense of frustration and alienation from the
creative CSSF process had terminal outcomes: the students disengaged with
the rehearsal process to such an extent that the group was forced to with-
draw from the project days before the final performance.

    It would be reductive and unfair to lay this withdrawal solely at the feet
of the identity dynamics within the group or Travis' pedagogical and
directorial decisions as discussed here. Nevertheless, from a student's com-
ments within the final focus group, there is a sense that more 'freedom' may
have facilitated a different outcome for the group:

> We need to be more free because, like, we should be allowed
> to laugh about a little bit . . . Because, we have to like put in
> all our feelings so much that we can't really express things,
> we have to think about . . . would he [Travis] like it if we say
> that? Or if I give a suggestion would it be alright? Like we
> can't be free.
> (Focus Group, 27 November 2013)

It is significant here that Sasheer states, 'we have to . . . put in all our feelings
so much' yet 'we can't really express things'. As Barnes discusses,

paternalistic and redemptive approaches to Shakespeare with diverse young people often require, or focus on the performance of, overt displays of emotionality, often connected to racialised or socio-economic trauma (Barnes 2020). This approach can be seen in Travis' focus on a performatively 'gritty' and 'urban' *Macbeth*. Sasheer's statement that the group needed 'to be more free . . . [and] allowed to laugh about a little' can be strongly contrasted with Grace's jocular rehearsal 'brackets', in which being free to be yourself and laugh about a bit is absolutely central. For Grace's student Arthur, the Shakespeare School Festival rehearsal room is a place to be yourself and share ideas in order to give you characters 'more personality'; while for Sasheer, Craig, Jack and James, it is a place to reproduce a preconceived persona, where laughter, expression and freedom risk their teachers' disapproval.

In this section, I have discussed the critical feminist pedagogy tradition of care- and identity-led teaching principles in drama education and active Shakespeare. In critically exploring one core active Shakespeare text's ambiguous positioning of identity within the practice, I have highlighted areas of further development, such as the use of conscious casting practices, intercultural communication and racial literacy training. Focusing on questions of care and identity within the collaborative active Shakespeare ensemble, I have contrasted how this can either be enacted or inhibited in practice via a comparative analysis of 'new paternalism' (Whitman 2008) with 'othermothering' (Henry 1992; Hughes 2019) approaches.

Whilst acknowledging where engaged specificity on identity-led Shakespeare work is lacking in the current active Shakespeare literature, I hope I have also shown how a consciously care- and identity-led approach is consistent with active Shakespeare principles and is currently being realised in practice in school contexts. In framing this analysis between 'new paternalism' and 'othermothering', I aim to recentralise the radical feminist pedagogy potential within active Shakespeare teaching and make an argument for its centrality in achieving the approach's social justice aims. In this, I seek to move away from more structural, theatre-civic models within active Shakespeare literature such as the Athenian *polis* (McGrath 2001), cited for example in Neelands' ensemble pedagogy writings

(Neelands 2009a), towards more consciously care-led models. The responsiveness and relationality of a 'care perspective' on civic imaginings holds opportunities for social justice–focused Shakespeare teaching unavailable in more formal and universalised 'justice perspectives' (Noddings 2013; Porter 1996).

In combination with 'playing the text' practices as explored in Section 3, care- and identity-led perspectives can, therefore, be seen as giving us the warp and weft of the critical active Shakespeare classroom, allowing the texts and learners to be fully present in all their complexity and variety. In the following section, I therefore turn to the critical possibilities and challenges of weaving these two threads together in the active Shakespeare classroom in such a way that continues to foreground the approach's social justice possibilities.

5 Critical Active Shakespeare as Restorying

In the previous two sections, I explored how the centrality of both play and care within active Shakespeare pedagogy can facilitate a fruitfully critical destabilisation of the text and an emancipatory centring of learners' identities and existing knowledges. As I have argued, existing active Shakespeare literature has focused largely on the explorative and destabilising value of playing and somewhat less fully, though still significantly, on the potential for identity-led approaches to active and embodied work. Yet, both are essential for an active Shakespeare pedagogy which is social justice–oriented.

In this concluding section, I discuss the potential and the imperative for 'story-weaving' in our Shakespeare teaching: using these two threads of playfully deconstructed text and the carefully valued identities and knowledges in the room to construct an understanding of Shakespeare which is nuanced, relevant and alive to contextual social justice issues. I explore how this story-weaving can be considered analogous to the critical pedagogy practice of 'restorying': the de-colonising practice of confronting and working through the exclusionary and colonial past (and present) of a text and retelling its story in a way that makes space for the knowledges, experiences and perspectives in the room. Using the materiality of the story-weaving metaphor, I explore where and how this restorying was both enacted and limited during the CSSF case studies. I emphasise, with reference back to the core critical pedagogy principle of social constructivism, how a commitment to restorying in active Shakespeare is distinct from viewing the play and care of active Shakespeare as an engaging 'opener', functioning to usher learners into a universalised comprehension and appreciation of Shakespeare. Restorying rather facilitates students' diverse connections *with* and contributions *to* the broader cultural ecology of multiple 'Shakespeares' conceived through scholarly study and performance. Finally, I draw this Element to a close by outlining my hopes for how future active and critical Shakespeare practice in schools, universities and community spaces might develop in light of this analysis.

As part of her discussion of multi-modal, collaborative literacy work as 'playing' the text, Mackey suggests the notion of 'weaving' a story as an analytic literary process: 'setting up the warp of interpretation so that the final texture can be woven using the specifics of the story as weft' (Mackey 2004: 240). This metaphor clearly demonstrates how the foundational playful and identity-led aspects of active Shakespeare pedagogy can be utilised and combined to construct rigorously text-based but authentically contextualised and resonant studies of the plays. The parallel, critical race pedagogy practice of 'restorying' is also relevant here.

Restorying – also referred to as counterstorying (Bissonnette & Glazier 2016; Dyches 2017; Dyches et al. 2021; Stornaiuolo & Thomas 2018) – can be understood as a process of re-articulating existing stories, texts and cultural objects 'to better reflect a diversity of perspectives and experiences, [and as] an act of asserting the importance of one's existence in a world that tries to silence subaltern voices' (Thomas & Stornaiuolo 2016). In Shakespeare education contexts, this describes a process of marginalised students discovering and developing 'an entry point into canonical conversations and a means by which to share and project their own experiential knowledge and lived experiences' (Dyches 2017: 317). Jeanne Dyches goes on to discuss in her paper the central social justice implications of this approach: allowing the students to centre themselves and their existing positionalities in their academic knowledge construction and develop a sense of autonomy and authority via the freedom to remake, reshape and transform texts through the resources available to them.

Restorying as an emancipatory educational practice highlights the discursive and explorative work of decolonising education. This framing advances the notion of decolonising beyond a common approach within literature and performing arts: focused on material questions of what texts to remove or add to a curriculum. As Hartley et al. emphasise in their study of decolonising Shakespeare through performance: 'decolonization is not merely about adding to or minimizing the influence of those things that have had the most colonial power. It is also about *radically remaking those culturally influential products in the image of the present*, assuming – of course – that we think there is still something of value to be made in the process' (Hartley et al. 2021: 176)

The notion of story-weaving and restorying, therefore, gives a concrete pedagogical metaphor for this processional aspect of decolonising practice around the teaching of Shakespeare. Active Shakespeare approaches, when following through on the rich possibilities of playing the word and the world of the text and of a mutually caring identity-led exploration of that text, are ideally placed to facilitate a Shakespeare education centred on restorying as its core process and outcome. Restorying – as an educational practice related to but distinct from creative practices of adaptation, appropriation, editing and translating – does not have to be radical or imply a complete re-writing or re-imagining of the text. As Amy Thomas and Ebony Elizabeth Stornaiuolo discuss in their study of young people's digital restorying practices, this work can appear 'minor' in execution but nevertheless represents powerful opportunities to push 'back on official interpretations to create counternarratives that assert, I exist, I matter, and I am here' (Thomas & Stornaiuolo 2016: 322). Within a restorying model of literary education, Shakespeare becomes, rather than an inert entity acting on the students, a potent source text for learners to actively speak through, speak with and speak against.

Within the CSSF case studies I observed, it was possible to see restorying of the text playing out in a variety of ways through the rehearsal and performance project. With Grace's students, as I have discussed throughout this Element, the combination of the project's 'playful ensemble' framing, alongside the care- and identity-led pedagogic work of the teacher, facilitated a contextualised and engaged interpretation of *Titus Andronicus* from the cast of 14–18 year olds. During the rehearsal process, the students' experiences of racism and colourism inform their analysis of race within *Titus*, in particular the position and fate of Aaron and Tamora's mixed race infant. The group was also frequently preoccupied with the violence of this play. In rehearsals, they were keen to explore how to temper the violence with tragic notions of 'care' and 'honour', as in Lavinia's death in the closing scene, or with a subversive sense of the carnivalesque, as in the scene of Titus' interaction with Tamora and her sons disguised as 'Murder', 'Rape' and 'Revenge'. During focus group sessions, the students reflected that this preoccupation was prompted by their own interests in relation to the play and the story of the text they wanted to tell their audience:

Jocelyn: But then like, with this one, with Titus, it's like, it's gory from the beginning, right until the end. It's just . . .

Eleanor: Yeah, I think it will make it more interesting for the people watching as well. Because they probably won't be expecting anything like that.

(Focus Group 1.2, 23 June 2014)

Amar: Like Grace said yeah . . . it was like bare violent. So from that we should learn that we have to make it appropriate for . . .

Nami: For our audience.

Amar: all age groups.

(Focus Group 1.1, 10 June 2014)

The cast expresses a desire to share a production of *Titus* which has the power to shock their audience of invited family and community members and potentially subvert their expectations of what a Shakespearean performance looks like, whilst also remaining careful of their young audience members – including siblings and relatives. While these rehearsal room explorations of race and violence in *Titus Andronicus* did not necessarily develop into a cohesive 'theme' for the production, they did signal an authentic and confident restorying encounter with the script, defined by the casts' own preoccupations with the text and their performance context. This can be understood as a restorying process led by 'playing the world' active practices, as discussed in Section 3. Through these open-ended but repeated returns to questions of race and violence in *Titus* during the rehearsal process, the cast and Grace are strengthening their story-weaving – returning to the themes and discourses of the play that hold significance for them, discussing them and exploring them through embodied performance contextualised in their own identities, knowledges and interests.

Another example of restorying could be seen in one of the pilot case studies, a South London all-girls Catholic School which took part in CSSF in 2013 as an extracurricular project open to all students. The play was *Much Ado About Nothing*, and, during rehearsals, the largely Afro-Caribbean cast members unsurprisingly took issue with the infamous line in which Claudio vows to take back his spurned bride Hero: 'I'll hold my mind, were she an Ethiope' (Act 5, scene 3, line 38). Teacher Lana facilitated a debate on this line's meaning and its appropriateness, taking into account that the other characters on stage at this point, Leonato, Antonio, Benedick, Beatrice, Friar Francis and Claudio, were all being played by black students to a white Hero. Exploring the potential implications and opportunities for dramaturgical commentary within this casting configuration, the group decided to mark the line with a drawn-out moment of disapproval from the other characters, in which they turn to Claudio and kiss their teeth. Claudio then, shame-faced and chastised, lowers his head for a beat before the action of the scene continues. Notably, teeth-kissing is a common expression of disapproval in many Afro-Caribbean cultures and one moreover frequently policed as 'disrespectful' and 'inappropriate' in many UK schools (Lough 2019). This is, therefore, a short but powerful piece of restorying, based within the active Shakespeare frame of 'playing the word'. The students react *both* in role as black-bodied Leonato, Antonio, Benedick, Beatrice and Friar Francis to Claudio's statement *and* as a young, racially diverse cast offering a narrative commentary on Shakespeare's writing framed in their own contemporary idiom. This restorying functions as a dramaturgical choice and meta-analysis of the text and its racial implications when rehearsed and performed in this South London community. And while it in no way neutralises the racism implicit in those words, through care and play, it creates space for a critical dialogue both in the rehearsal room and performance.

In active Shakespeare work which leads to performance projects such as those described earlier, it is perhaps easy to see how active and performative approaches *can* facilitate restorying. The act of bringing these words to life with our voices and bodies, implicated as they are in identity positionalities and power ecologies, forensically brings to the fore questions of social and post-colonial justice in how we interpret and perform the text. However, this is not to suggest that only public performance-focused active Shakespeare work can support restorying practices. In recent Shakespeare education literature, there are examples of in-class adaptations of scenes and texts supporting a critical reading of multiple editions of the plays for undergraduate students (Dawson 2009; Dolan 2009). However, in *Teaching Shakespeare with Purpose* in particular, there is a wide range of examples in the final chapter on fusing active and discursive approaches with written and creative assessments which supports a contextualised restorying approach to the texts (Thompson & Turchi 2016).

Returning to the core critical pedagogy commitment to knowledge as a social construct, what ultimately defines these restorying approaches is their whole-hearted commitment to a key shift within Shakespeare studies more broadly. As Shakespeare education scholar Kate Flaherty argues, this is a move away from 'Shakespeare' as a single, holistic, cultural and textual object towards multiple 'Shakespeares' predicated 'upon possibilities of embodied rhetoric, upon the collaborative, creative and culturally situated practices of interpretation, and particularly [learners'] vivid lives in the present' (Flaherty 2013: 77). As Flaherty emphasises, this shift within Shakespeare scholarship holds key implications for Shakespeare pedagogy which, as I have argued throughout this Element, the playful and careful practices of active Shakespeare can help us attune to in material and embodied ways.

Flaherty frames a useful line of argument here when she writes of the importance of 'local Shakespeares'. Speaking of the value of drawing on Australian theatre productions of Shakespeare in an Australian teaching context, Flaherty states: 'Local Shakespeares are not just distant iterations of the real subject of scholarly attention but are, much more compellingly, by their very locality, constitutive of the dynamic cultural field called "Shakespeare"' (Flaherty 2013: 75)

This commitment to viewing the work in each of our Shakespeare contexts and classrooms not as becoming aware of or critically appreciating a distant and centralised field of Shakespeare studies, but being *actual enactments* of it, is central to the knowledge-production commitment which runs through active Shakespeare pedagogy. Viewed through a lens of social power ecologies (Massey 2005), this is about the difference between passively inculcating our students to accept existing webs of power as naturalised and universal and consciously working to develop an awareness of these webs of power and facilitating learners' active work within them, through the rich and knotty lens of Shakespeare's texts and cultural positionality. Several contributors to recent Shakespeare education books make statements demonstrating the nature of this commitment: 'Our knowledge changes constantly. We don't just transmit a stable body of knowledge, because it doesn't exist. We constantly remake it and we do so in a collaborative way' (Dolan 2009: 189) My relationship with my students in class was now that of teacher, director, fellow actor – *collaborator*' (Homan 2019a: 87) Increasingly, I find I am not so much "delivering" Shakespeare to my heterogeneous and ethically/racially diverse student population as I am tapping into what they already know, experientially, in order to clear a path for them to forge their own connections' (Conn Liebler 2019: 173)

This perspective can be compared to the principles of student-as-producer (Lambert 2009; Neary et al. 2014; Winn 2015), a movement within higher education which view students not as 'deficient' learners but as incoming co-producers of knowledge and emerging members of the academy's community of practice (Krajcik et al. 2007; Mahon et al. 2019; Murray 2012). At the University of Warwick, the potential of active, embodied and drama-based pedagogies to facilitate this egalitarian and collaborative educational approach has been explored through the concept of 'Open Space Learning' (Monk et al. 2011a). Through an analysis of Open Space Learning practices across a variety of departments, including Law, English and Education, Monk et al. explore the potential this embodied and drama-focused work held for creating 'trans' spaces – liminal spaces of possibility for social change and resistance as well as curriculum-focused knowledge creation. While this is a principle developed in the context of higher education, where the notion of learner as co-creator is perhaps not so challenging due to the age and stage of the learners in question, some of whom may only be a few years from the start of their own research careers, I would suggest it is equally valid within a school-age context. With its grounding in the collaborative and discursive 'living through' practices of process drama (Bowell & Heap 2001), radical emancipatory strategies of forum theatre (Boal 2006) and inspiration from the explorative world-making work of the professional rehearsal room (Neelands & O'Hanlon 2011), the critical legacy of theatre and drama in education within active Shakespeare can be a potent and engaging tool to facilitate the egalitarian student-as-producer principles of restorying at all educational levels.

Throughout this Element, I have aimed to take a clear-eyed perspective on the implications and challenges of viewing active Shakespeare teaching practice as a critical pedagogy approach: acknowledging the limitations and gaps of its twentieth-century literature and outlining the potential of recentring the practice's critical pedagogy legacy for the social justice–focused demands of twenty-first-century Shakespeare teaching and learning. The recent convergences around drama education, Shakespeare pedagogy and performance, and questions of decolonisation and social justice (Eklund & Hyman 2019; Freebody & Finneran 2021; Jarrett-Macauley 2017; Ruiter 2020a) suggest rich opportunities for further collaboration and development within this multidisciplinary field of scholarship and practice. In mapping out the ideas and case study vignettes of this Element, it is my hope to speak to a range of Shakespeare education audiences. Firstly, to prompt active Shakespeare proponents and practitioners to draw further and more nuanced inspiration from critical, critical race and feminist pedagogies. Secondly, to inspire critical and social justice–focused Shakespeare educators and scholars to explore the potential of active, theatre-based practice in their teaching. And finally, to welcome and engage developments in diverse and critical contemporary Shakespeare performance practice in to educational contexts at all ages and stages.

References

Adams, B. K. (2021). This truly expresses how I decenter Shakespeare in my research and want to introduce students to him with a grain of salt. 24 March 2021, https://twitter.com/bkadams/status/1367267574078201857.

Adams Jr, C. N. (2013). TIE and critical pedagogy. In A. Jackson & C. Vine, eds., *Learning Through Theatre: The Changing Face of Theatre in Education*, 3rd ed., London: Routledge, pp. 287–304.

Aitken, V. (2009). Conversations with status and power: How everyday theatre offers 'spaces of agency' to participants. *Research in Drama Education: The Journal of Applied Theatre and Performance*, 14(4), 503–27.

Allen, R. L. (2004). Whiteness and critical pedagogy. *Educational Philosophy and Theory*, 36(2), 121–36.

Anderson, M. & J. Dunn (eds.) (2013). *How Drama Activates Learning: Contemporary Research and Practice*, London: Bloomsbury.

Araki-Metcalfe, N. (2008). Introducing creative language learning in Japan through educational drama. *NJ: Drama Australia Journal*, 31(2), 45–57.

Babulski, T. (2020). Being and becoming woke in teacher education. *Phenomenology & Practice*, 14(1), 73–88.

Baines, D. (2013). Social justice politics: Care as democracy and resistance. In K. Freebody, S. Goodwin & H. Proctor, eds., *Higher Education, Pedagogy and Social Justice*, Cham: Palgrave Macmillan, pp. 67–80.

Bakhtin, M. (1984). *Rabelais and His World*, Bloomington: Indiana University Press.

Bala, S. & A. I. Albacan (2013). Workshopping the revolution? On the phenomenon of joker training in the theatre of the oppressed. *Research in Drama Education: The Journal of Applied Theatre and Performance*, 18(4), 388–402.

Banks, F. (2014). *Creative Shakespeare: The Globe Education Guide to Practical Shakespeare*, London: Bloomsbury.

Barnden, S. (2021). I took a picture of the poster for the BL's Shakespeare exhibition to make a cheap joke on Facebook and then ended up writing about it in my book. 24 March 2021, https://twitter.com/sally_barn den/status/1367084027228942342.

Barnes, T. L. (2020). *Shakespearean Charity and the Perils of Redemptive Performance*, Cambridge: Cambridge University Press. https://doi.org/10.1017/9781108785716.

Bate, J. (1997). *The Genius of Shakespeare*, London: Picador.

Baxter, J. (2002). A juggling act: A feminist post-structuralist analysis of girls' and boys' talk in the secondary classroom. *Gender and Education*, 14(1), 5–19.

Baxter, J. (2015). Who wants to be the leader? Linguistic construction of emerging leadership in differently gendered teams. *International Journal of Business Communication*, 52(2), 427–51.

Berry, C. (2004). *Working Shakespeare*, New York: The Working Arts Library.

Berry, C. (2008). *From Word to Play: A Textual Handbook for Directors and Actors*, London: Oberon Books.

Bhabha, H. K. (2004). *The Location of Culture*, London: Psychology Press.

Biggers, J. (2012). The 'madness' of the Tucson book ban: Interview with Mexican American studies teacher Curtis Acosta on *The Tempest*. 6 July 2022, www.huffingtonpost.com/jeff-biggers/tucson-ethnic-studies_b_1210393.html.

Bissonnette, J. D. & J. Glazier (2016). A counterstory of one's own: Using counterstory telling to engage students with the British canon. *Journal of Adolescent and Adult Literacy*, 59(6), 685–94.

Blank, P. (2014). Introducing 'interlinguistics': Shakespeare and early/modern English. In M. Saenger, ed., *Interlinguicity, Internationality and Shakespeare*, Montreal: McGill-Queens University Press, pp. 138–58.

Boal, A. (2006). *The Aesthetics of the Oppressed*, London: Routledge.

Bolton, G. (1986). The activity of dramatic playing. In D. Davis & C. Lawrence, eds., *Gavin Bolton: Selected Writings*, New York: Longman.

Bolton, G. (1998). *Acting in Classroom Drama: A Critical Analysis*, Stoke-on-Trent: Trentham.

Bowell, P. & Heap, B. (2001). *Planning Process Drama*, London: Fulton.

Boyd, M. (2 April 2009). Building relationships. *The Stage*.

Bruner, J. S. (1972). Nature and uses of immaturity. *American Psychologist*, 27, 687–708.

Bruner, J. S. (2006). *In Search of Pedagogy Volume I: The Selected Works of Jerome S. Bruner*, London: Routledge.

Caldwell Cook, H. (1917). *The Play Way; an Essay in Educational Method*, New York: Frederick A. Stokes Company.

Castoriadis, C. (1997). *The Castoriadis Reader*. (D. A. Curtis, Ed.), Oxford: Blackwell.

Cavendish, D. (2020). The woke brigade are close to 'cancelling' Shakespeare. *Telegraph*, 9 February, London.

Cheng, A. Y. & J. Winston (2011). Shakespeare as a second language: Playfulness, power and pedagogy in the ESL classroom. *Research in Drama Education: The Journal of Applied Theatre*, 16(4), 37–41.

Cho, S. (2016). Critical pedagogy, historical origins of. *Encyclopedia of Educational Philosophy and Theory*, pp. 1–6.

Coles, J. (2013). 'Every child's birthright'? Democratic entitlement and the role of canonical literature in the English national curriculum. *Curriculum Journal*, 24(1), 50–66.

Conn Liebler, N. (2019). 'Whos there?' 'nay, answer me. Stand and unfold yourself': Attending to students in diversified settings. In S. Homan, ed., *How and Why We Teach Shakespeare: College Teachers and Directors Share How They Explore the Playwright's Works with Their Students*, New York: Routledge, pp. 171–9.

Cook, G. (2000). *Language Play, Language Learning*, Oxford: Oxford University Press.

Courtney, R. (1990). *Drama and Intelligence a Cognitive Theory*, Montreal: McGill-Queens University Press.

Dadabhoy, A. & N. Mehdizadeh (2020). Cultivating and anti-racist pedagogy. 21 August 2020, https://youtu.be/_4oCWstlcPc.

Dawson, A. B. (2009). Teaching the script. In G. B. Shand, ed., *Teaching Shakespeare: Passing It On*, Oxford: Wiley-Blackwell, pp. 75–90.

de Jong, S., R. Icaza & O. U. Rutazibwa (eds.) (2019). *Decolonization and Feminisms in Global Teaching and Learning*, London: Routledge.

Delamont, S. (2014). Research on classroom interaction: The spectrum since 1970. *Research Intelligence: News from the British Educational Research Association*, 123, 14–15.

Della Gatta, C. (2019). Confronting bias and identifying facts: Teaching resistance through Shakespeare. In H. Eklund & W. B. Hyman, eds., *Teaching Social Justice Through Shakespeare: Why Renaissance Literature Matters Now*, Edinburgh: Edinburgh University Press, pp. 165–73.

Desai, A. N. (2019). Topical Shakespeare and the urgency of ambiguity. In W. B. Hyman & H. Eklund, eds., *Teaching Social Justice Through Shakespeare: Why Renaissance Literature Matters Now*, Edinburgh: Edinburgh University Press, pp. 27–35.

Dewey, J. (1916). *Education and Democracy*, New York: The Free Press.

Dolan, F. E. (2009). Learning to listen: Shakespeare and contexts. In G. B. Shand, ed., *Teaching Shakespeare: Passing It On*, Oxford: Wiley-Blackwell.

Dolan, J. (2006). Utopia in performance. *Theatre Research International*, 31(2), 163–73.

Dunn, J. (2010). Child-structured socio-dramatic play and the drama educator. In S. Schonmann, ed., *Key Concepts in Theatre/Drama Education*, Rotterdam: Sense, pp. 29–33.

Dyches, J. (2017). Shaking off Shakespeare: A white teacher, urban students, and the mediating powers of a canonical counter-curriculum. *Urban Review*, 49(2), 300–25.

Dyches, J., A. S. Boyd & J. M. Schulz (2021). Critical content knowledges in the English language arts classroom: Examining practicing teachers' nuanced perspectives. *Journal of Curriculum Studies*, 53(3), 1–17.

Eklund, H. & W. B. Hyman (eds.) (2019). *Teaching Social Justice Through Shakespeare: Why Renaissance Literature Matters Now*, Edinburgh: Edinburgh University Press.

Ellsworth, E. (1989). Why doesn't this feel empowering?: Working through the repressive myths of critical pedagogy. *Harvard Educational Review*, 59(3), 297–325.

Equity and Directors Guild of Great Britain. (2004). Ensemble Theatre Conference, 23 November, *The Pit, The Barbican, London*, London: Equity and Directors Guild of Great Britain.

Espinosa, R. (2019a). Chicano Shakespeare: The bard, the border, and the peripheries of performance. In H. Eklund & W. B. Hyman, eds., *Teaching Social Justice Through Shakespeare: Why Renaissance Literature Matters Now*, Edinburgh: Edinburgh University Press, pp. 76–84.

Espinosa, R. (2019b). Shakespeare and your mountainish inhumanity. 1 February 2021, https://medium.com/the-sundial-acmrs/shakespeare-and-your-mountainish-inhumanity-d255474027de.

Etheridge Woodson, S. (2015). *Theatre for Youth Third Space: Performance, Democracy and Community Cultural Development*, Bristol: Intellect.

Finlay-Johnson, H. (1912). *The Dramatic Method of Teaching*, London: Nisbet Press.

Finneran, M. (2008). Critical myths in drama as education. PhD thesis. The University of Warwick.

Finneran, M. & K. Freebody (eds.) (2016). *Drama and Social Justice: Theory, Research and Practice in International Contexts*, London: Routledge.

Flaherty, K. (2013). Habitation and naming: Teaching local Shakespeares. In K. Flaherty, P. Gay & L. E. Semler, eds., *Teaching Shakespeare Beyond the Centre Australasian Perspectives*, Basingstoke: Palgrave Macmillan, pp. 75–86.

Flaherty, K., P. Gay & L. E. Semler (2013). *Teaching Shakespeare Beyond the Centre: Australasian Perspectives*, Basingstoke: Palgrave Macmillan. https://doi.org/10.1057/9781137275073.

Fleming, M. (2010). *Arts in Education and Creativity: A Literature Review*, Newcastle: Creativity, Culture and Education.

Folger Shakespeare Library (2021). Folger critical race conversations event series. 26 July 2021, www.folger.edu/critical-race-conversations.

Foucault, M. (1975). *Discipline and Punish*, New York: Random House.

Foucault, M. (1978). *The History of Sexuality: An Introduction*, Harmondsworth: Penguin.

Freebody, K. & M. Finneran (2013). Drama and social justice: Power, participation and possibility the key terms. In J. Dunn & M. Anderson, eds., *How Drama Activates Learning: Contemporary Research and Practice*, London: Bloomsbury.

Freebody, K. & M. Finneran (2021). *Critical Themes in Drama: Social, Cultural and Political Analysis*, Oxford: Routledge.

Freebody, K., M. Finneran, M. Balfour & M. Anderson (eds.) (2018). *Applied Theatre: Understanding Change*, London: Springer.

Freire, P. (1972). *Pedagogy of the Oppressed*, London: Penguin.

Freire, P. (2000). *Pedagogy of Hope*, London: Continuum.

Freire, P. (2016). *Pedagogy of the Heart*, London: Bloomsbury.

Gallagher, K. (2006). (Post)Critical ethnography in drama research. In J. Ackroyd, ed., *Research Methodologies for Drama Education*, Stoke-on-Trent: Trentham Books, pp. 63–80.

Gallagher, K. (2015). Beckoning hope and care. *Research in Drama Education: The Journal of Applied Theatre and Performance*, 20(3), 422–5.

Gallagher, K. (2016a). Can a classroom be a family? Race, space, and the labour of care in urban teaching. *Canadian Journal of Education*, 39(2), 1–36.

Gallagher, K. (2016b). Responsible art and unequal societies: Towards a theory of drama and the justice agenda. In K. Freebody & M. Finneran, eds., *Drama and Social Justice: Theory, Research and Practice in International Contexts*, London: Routledge, pp. 53–66.

Gallagher, K. (2016c). The micro-political and the socio-structural in applied theatre with homeless youth. In J. Hughes & H. Nicholson, eds., *Critical Perspectives on Applied Theatre*, Cambridge: Cambridge University Press, pp. 229–47.

Gallagher, K. (2017). The gendered labor of social innovation: Theatre, pedagogy, and the girl-child in India. *Review of Education, Pedagogy, and Cultural Studies*, 39(5), 470–85.

Gallagher, K. & K. Jacobson (2018). Beyond mimesis to an assemblage of reals in the drama classroom: Which reals? Which representational aesthetics? What theatre-building practices? Whose truths? *Research in Drama Education: The Journal of Applied Theatre and Performance*, 23(1), 40–55.

Gallagher, K., N. Cardwell, R. Rhoades & S. Bie (2017). Drama in Education and Applied Theater, from Morality and Socialization to Play and Postcolonialism. *Oxford Research Encyclopedia of Education*. https:doi.org/10.1093/acrefore/9780190264093.013.34.

Gallagher, K. & D. J. Rodricks (2017). Hope despite hopelessness: Race, gender, and the pedagogies of drama/applied theatre as a relational ethic in neoliberal times. *Youth Theatre Journal*, 31(2), 114–28.

Gallagher, K., D. J. Rodricks & K., Jacobson (eds.) (2020). *Global Youth Citizenry and Radical Hope*, Singapore: Springer.

Gallagher, K., B. Y. Ntelioglou & A. Wessels (2013). 'Listening to the affective life of injustice': Drama pedagogy, race, identity, and learning. *Youth Theatre Journal*, 27(1), 7–19. https://doi.org/10.1080/08929092.2013.779349.

Gallagher, M. (2008). 'Power is not an evil': Rethinking power in participatory methods. *Children's Geographies*, 6(2), 137–50.

Gerzic, M. & A. Norrie (eds.) (2020). *Playfulness in Shakespearean Adaptations*, London: Routledge.

Gibson, R. (2016). *Teaching Shakespeare: A Handbook for Teachers*, 2nd ed., Cambridge: Cambridge University Press.

Giroux, H. (1997). *Pedagogy and the Politics of Hope: Theory, Culture and Schooling: A Critical Reader*, Boulder: Westview Press.

Golsby-Smith, S. (2013). 'Let me be that I am': The rhetoric of the teenage self and Shakespeare in performance. In K. Flaherty, P. Gay & L. E. Semler, eds., *Teaching Shakespeare Beyond the Centre: Australasian Perspectives*, Basingstoke: Palgrave Macmillan, pp. 125–36.

Grady, S. (2003). Accidental Marxists? The challenge of critical and feminist pedagogies for the practice of applied drama. *Youth Theatre Journal*, 17(1), 65–81.

Green, J. M. (2008). *Pragmatism and Social Hope: Deepening Democracy in Global Contexts*, New York: Columbia University Press.

Greene, M. (1987). Creating, experiencing, sense-making: Art worlds in schools. *Journal of Aesthetic Education*, 21(4), 11–23.

Hall, K. F. (1995). *Things of Darkness: Economies of Race and Gender in Early Modern England*, Ithaca: Cornell University Press.

Hall, K. F. (1998). 'These bastard signs of fair': Literary whiteness in Shakespeare's sonnets. In A. Loomba & M. Orkin, eds., *Post-Colonial Shakespeares*, New York: Routledge, pp. 64–83.

Hargreaves, D. H. (1997). In defence of research for evidence-based teaching: A rejoinder to Martyn Hammersley. *British Educational Research Journal*, 23(4), 405–19.

Hartley, A. J., K. Dunn & C. Berry (2021). Pedagogy: Decolonizing Shakespeare on stage. In D. Ruiter, ed., *The Arden Research Handbook of Shakespeare and Contemporary Performance*, London: Bloomsbury Arden Shakespeare, pp. 171–91. https://doi.org/10.5040/9781350080706.ch-2.7.

Harvie, J. (2011). Democracy and neoliberalism in art's social turn and Roger Hiorns's *Seizure*. *Performance Research*, 16(2), 113–23.

Hatfull, R. & T. Mookherjee (2021). *Fracking Shakespeare Seminar*, Athens: European Shakespeare Research Association.

Henry, A. (1992). African Canadian women teachers' activism: Recreating communities of caring and resistance. *The Journal of Negro Education*, 61(3), 392–404.

Heron, J. & N. Johnson (2017). Critical pedagogies and the theatre laboratory. *Research in Drama Education: The Journal of Applied Theatre and Performance*, 22(2), 282–7. https://doi.org/10.1080/13569783.2017.1293513.

Hobgood, A. P. (2019). Shakespeare in Japan: Disability and a pdagogy of disorientation. In H. Eklund & W. B. Hyman, eds., *Teaching Social Justice Through Shakespeare: Why Renaissance Literature Matters Now*, Edinburgh: University of Edinburgh Press, pp. 46–54.

Holdsworth, N. (2007). Spaces to play/playing with spaces: Young people, citizenship and Joan Littlewood. *Research in Drama Education*, 12(3), 293–304.

Holligan, C. (2010). Building one-dimensional places: Death by the power of audit. *Power and Education*, 2(3), 288–99.

Homan, S. (2019a). 'Gladly would he learn and gladly teach': Empowering students with Shakespeare. In S. Homan, ed., *How and Why We Teach Shakespeare: College Teachers and Directors Share How They Explore the Playwright's Works with Their Students*, Oxford: Routledge, pp. 65–74.

Homan, S. (ed.) (2019b). *How and Why We Teaching Shakespeare: College Teachers and Directors Share How They Explore the Playwright's Works with Their Students*, Oxford: Routledge.

Hooks, B. (1994). *Teaching to Transgress: Education as the Practice of Freedom*, London: Routledge.

Hooks, b. (2003). *Teaching Community: A Pedagogy of Hope*, Oxford: Routledge.

Hornbrook, D. (1998). *Education and Dramatic Art*, 2nd ed., London: Routledge.

Hughes, J. & H. Nicholson (eds.) (2016). *Critical Perspectives on Applied Theatre*, Cambridge: Cambridge University Press.

Hughes, K. A. (2019). Black Narcissus: The role of the suburban other-mother. PhD thesis. University of Michigan-Dearborn.

Huizinga, J. (1949). *Homo Ludens: A Study of the Play Element in Culture*, London: Temple Smith.

Hulme, R., D. Cracknell & A. Owens (2009). Learning in third spaces: Developing trans-professional understanding through practitioner enquiry. *Educational Action Research*, 17(4), 537–50.

Hunka, E. (2015). It feels like home: The role of the aesthetic space in participatory work with vulnerable children. *Research in Drama Education: The Journal of Applied Theatre and Performance*, 20(3), 293–7.

Hunter, M. A. (2008). Cultivating the art of safe space. *Research in Drama Education: The Journal of Applied Theatre and Performance*, 13(1), 5–21.

Hytten, K. (2011). Building and sustaining hope: A response to 'meaningful hope for teachers in a time of high anxiety and low morale'. *Democracy & Education*, 19(1), 1–3.

Irish, T. (2008). Teaching Shakespeare: A history of the teaching of Shakespeare in England, Stratford-upon-Avon: Royal Shakespeare, p. 16.

Irish, T. (2016). Possible Shakespeares: The educational value of working with Shakespeare through theatre-based practice. PhD thesis. The University of Warwick.

Jarrett-Macauley, D. (ed.) (2017). *Shakespeare, Race and Performance: The Diverse Bard*, New York: Routledge.

Julian, E. & K. Solga (2021). Ethics: The challenge of practising (and not just representing) diversity at the Stratford Festival of Canada. In P. Kirwan & K. Prince, eds., *The Arden Research Handbook of Shakespeare and Contemporary Performance*, London: The Arden Shakespeare, pp. 192–210.

Kemmis, S. & T. Smith (2008). Praxis and Praxis development. In S. Kemmis & T. Smith, eds., *Enabling Praxis: Challenges for Education*, Rotterdam: Sense, pp. 23–13.

Kemp, S. (2019). Shakespeare in transition: Pedagogies of transgender justice. In H. Eklund & W. B. Hyman, eds., *Teaching Social Justice Through Shakespeare: Why Renaissance Literature Matters Now*, Edinburgh: University of Edinburgh Press, pp. 36–45.

Kincheloe, J. L. (2008). *Critical Pedagogy Primer*, 2nd ed., New York: Peter Lang.

Kitchen, J. (2015). The ensemble domesticated: Mapping issues of autonomy and power in performing arts projects in schools. *Power and Education*, 7(1), 90–105.

Kitchen, J. (2018). Playfulness in performative approaches to teaching Shakespeare. In O. Mentz & M. Fleiner, eds., *The Arts in Language*

Teaching. International Perspectives: Performative – Aesthetic – Transversal, Berlin: LIT Verlag, pp. 212–30.

Kitchen, J. (2021). Theatre and drama education and populism: The ensemble 'family' as a space for dialogic empathy and civic care. *British Educational Research Journal*, 47(2), 372–88.

Kitchen, J. (2022). Shakespeare youth performance festivals as spaces for postcolonial restorying. In S. Busby, K. Freebody & C. Rajendran, eds., *Routledge Companion to Theatre and Young People*, London: Routledge, pp. 84–101.

Klein, M. (1998). How teacher subjectivity in teaching mathematics-as-usual disenfranchises students, Nottingham: Paper presented to Mathematics Education and Society: An International Conference.

Krajcik, J., K. McNeill & B. Reiser (2007). Becoming a scientist: The role of undergraduate research in students' cognitive, personal, and professional development. *Science Education*, 91(1), 36–74.

Lambert, C. (2009). Pedagogies of participation in higher education: A case for research based learning. *Pedagogy, Culture and Society*, 17(3), 295–309.

Leonardo, Z. (2002). The souls of white folk: Critical pedagogy, whiteness studies, and globalisation discourse. *Race Ethnicity and Education*, 5(1), 29–50.

Lighthill, B. (2011). 'Shakespeare' – an endangered species? *English in Education*, 45(1), 36–51.

Loomba, A. (1989). *Gender, Race, Renaissance Drama*, Manchester: Manchester University Press.

Lough, C. (2019). Detention for kissing teeth 'risks racial harassment'. *Times Educational Supplement Magazine*. 18 October. www.tes.com/news/detention-kissing-teeth-risks-racial-harassment.

Luke, C. (1992). Feminist politics in radical pedagogy. In C. Luke & J. Gore, eds., *Feminisms and Critical Pedagogy*, New York: Routledge, pp. 25–53.

MacFaul, T. (2015). *Shakespeare's Animals*, Oxford: University of Oxford.

Mackey, M. (2004). Playing the text. In T. Grainger, ed., *The Routledge Falmer Reader in Language and Literacy*, London: Routledge Falmer, pp. 236–52.

Mahon, K., H. L. T. Heikkinen & R. Huttunen (2019). Critical educational praxis in university ecosystems: Enablers and constraints. *Pedagogy, Culture and Society*, 27(3), 463–80.

Massey, D. (2005). *For Space*, London: Sage.

Mayo, C. & N. M. Rodriguez (eds.) (2019). *Queer Pedagogies: Theory, Praxis, Politics*, Cham: Springer. https://doi.org/10.1002/9781119315049.ch7.

McCarthy, H. R. (2021). Leave to Speak: White scholars, 'allyship', and Shakespeare studies. *Shakespeare*, 17(1), 134–42.

McGrath, J. (2001). Theatre and democracy. *European Studies*, 17, 133–9.

McLuskie, K. (2009). Dancing and thinking: Teaching 'Shakespeare' in the twenty-first century. In G. B. Shand, ed., *Teaching Shakespeare: Passing It On*, Chichester: Wiley-Blackwell, pp. 132–41.

Monchinski, T. (2008). *Critical Pedagogy and the Everyday Classroom*, New York: Springer. https://doi.org/10.1007/978-1-4020-8463-8.

Monk, N., C. C. Rutter, J. Neelands & J. Heron (2011a). *Open Space Learning: A Study in Transdisciplinary Pedagogy*, London: Bloomsbury.

Monk, N., J. Heron, J. Neelands & C. C. Rutter (2011b). Learning to play with Shakespeare. In N. Monk, C. C. Rutter, J. Neelands & J. Heron (eds.), *Open Space Learning: A Study in Transdisciplinary Pedagogy*, London: Bloomsbury, pp. 57–91.

Murray, R. (2012). Developing a community of research practice. *British Educational Research Journal*, 38(5), 783–800.

Neary, M., G. Saunders, A. Hagyard & D. Derricott (2014). *Student as Producer: Research-Engaged Teaching, an Institutional Strategy.* New York: Higher Education Academy.

Neelands, J. (2004). Miracles are happening: Beyond the rhetoric of transformation in the Western traditions of drama education. *Research in Drama Education: The Journal of Applied Theatre and Performance*, 9(1), 47–56.

Neelands, J. (2008). Neelands in role as Cordelia. 25 May 2021, https://youtu.be/QYgwefDG0YM.

Neelands, J. (2009a). Acting together: Ensemble as a democratic process in art and life. *Research in Drama Education: The Journal of Applied Theatre and Performance*, 14(2), 173–89.

Neelands, J. (2009b). The Art of togetherness: Reflections on some essential artistic and pedagogic qualities of drama curricula. *NJ: Drama Australia Journal*, 33(1), 9–18.

Neelands, J. (2010a). 11/9 – The space in our hearts. In P. O'Connor, ed., *Creating Democratic Citizenship through Drama Education: The Writings of Jonothan Neelands*, Stoke-on-Trent: Trentham Books, pp. 119–30.

Neelands, J. (2010b). *Creating Democratic Citizenship Through Drama Education: The Writings of Jonothan Neelands*. Stoke-on-Trent: Trentham Books.

Neelands, J. (2010c). Mirror, dynamo or lens? Drama, children and social change. In P. O'Connor, ed., *Creating Democratic Citizenship through Drama Education*, Stoke-on-Trent: Trentham Books, pp. 143–58.

Neelands, J. (2016). Democratic and participatory theatre for social justice. In K. Freebody & M. Finneran, eds., *Drama and Social Justice: Theory, Research and Practice in International Contexts*, London: Routledge, pp. 30–9.

Neelands, J. & J. O'Hanlon (2011). There is some soul of good: An action-centred approach to teaching Shakespeare in schools. *Shakespeare Survey*, 64, 240–50.

Nelson, B. (2011a). 'I made myself': Playmaking as a pedagogy of change with urban youth. *Research in Drama Education: The Journal of Applied Theatre and Performance*, 16(2), 157–72.

Nelson, B. (2011b). Power and community in drama. In S. Schonmann, ed., *Key Concepts in Theatre/Drama Education*, Rotterdam: Sense, pp. 81–5.

Nicholson, H. (2011). *Theatre, Education and Performance*, Hampshire: Palgrave Macmillan.

Noddings, N. (2013). *Caring: A Relational Approach to Ethics and Moral Education*, 2nd ed., Los Angeles: University of California Press.

Nolan, C. & S. M. Stitzlein (2011). Meaningful hope for teachers in times of high anxiety and low morale. *Democracy & Education*, 19(1), 1–10.

NotAnotherShakespearePodcast. (2020). Takes neither itself nor Shakespeare seriously. Hosts: Nora (theatre nerd/Shax expert) & James (husband/theatre skeptic). 24 March 2021, https://twitter.com/NAShaxPodcast.

O'Brien, P., J. Addison Roberts, M. Tolaydo & N. Goodwin (eds.) (2006). *Shakespeare Set Free: Teaching* a Midsummer Night's Dream, Romeo and Juliet *and* Macbeth: *An Innovative, Performance-based Approach to Teaching Shakespeare*, 2nd ed., New York: Washington Square Press.

O'Connor, P. (2014). Drama as critical pedagogy: Re-imagining terrorism. In J. Dunn & M. Anderson, eds., *How Drama Activates Learning: Contemporary Research and Practice*, London: Bloomsbury, pp. 125–34. https://doi.org/10.5040/9781472553010.ch-009.

O'Connor, P. (2016). Moments of beauty and resistance through drama education. In K. Freebody & M. Finneran, eds., *Drama and Social Justice: Theory, Research and Practice in International Contexts*, London: Routledge, pp. 133–42.

O'Connor, P. & M. Anderson (2015). *Applied Theatre Research: Radical Departures*, London: Bloomsbury.

O'Dair, S. & T. Francisco (eds.) (2019). *Shakespeare and the 99%: Literary Studies, the Profession, and the Production of Inequity*, Cham: Palgrave Macmillan.

O'Toole, J. (2001). Pilgrim's Progress. In B. Rasmussen & A. Østern, eds., *Playing Betwixt and between, the IDEA Dialogues, 2000*, Oslo: Idea, pp. 93–9.

O'Toole, J. (2010). A preflective keynote: IDIERI 2009. *Research in Drama Education: The Journal of Applied Theatre and Performance*, 15(2), 271–92.

Olive, S. (2011). The Royal Shakespeare Company as 'cultural chemist': Critiquing the notion of Shakespeare as a 'cultural catalyst'. In P. Holland, ed., *Shakespeare Survey*, Vol. 64, Cambridge: Cambridge University Press, pp. 51–259.

Piaget, J. (1962). *Play, Dreams and Imitation in Childhood*, New York: Norton.

Pigkou-Repousi, M. (2012). Ensemble theatre and citizenship education: How ensemble theatre contributes to citizenship education. PhD thesis. University of Warwick.

Pigkou-Repousi, M. (2020). The politics of care in indifferent times: Youth narratives, caring practices, and transformed discourses in Greek education amid economic and refugee crises. In K. Gallagher, D. J. Rodricks & K. Jacobson, eds., *Global Youth Citizenry and Radical Hope: Enacting Community-Engaged Research through Performative Methodologies*, Singapore: Springer, pp. 111–34.

Pittard, E. (2015). Who does critical pedagogy think you are? Investigating how teachers are produced in critical pedagogy scholarship to inform teacher education. *Pedagogies: An International Journal*, 10(4), 328–48.

Porter, E. (1996). Women and friendships: Pedagogies of care and relationality. In C. Luke, ed., *Feminisms and Pedagogies of Everyday Life*, New York: State University of New York Press, pp. 57–80.

Pullman, P. (2014). Patron statement. 4 July 2014, www.shakespeareschools.org/about-us/patrons.

Rajendran, C. (2014). Acting as agency: Re-connecting selves and others in multicultural Singapore. *Theatre, Dance and Performance Training*, 5(2), 169–80.

Rajendran, C. (2016). Multicultural play as 'open culture' in 'safe precincts': Making space for difference in youth theatre. *Research in Drama Education: The Journal of Applied Theatre and Performance*, 21(4), 443–58.

Roche, J. (2007). Socially engaged art, critics and discontents: An interview with Claire Bishop. Community Arts Network Reading Room, July. June 2010. www.communityarts.net/readingroom/archivefiles/2006/07/socially_engage.php.

Rocklin, E. L. (2005). *Performance Approaches to Teaching Shakespeare*, Urbana: National Council of Teachers of English.

Rodricks, D. J. (2015). Drama education as 'restorative' for the third space. *Research in Drama Education: The Journal of Applied Theatre and Performance*, 20(3), 340–3.

Rohrer, J. (2018). 'It's in the room': Reinvigorating feminist pedagogy, contesting neoliberalism, and trumping post-truth populism. *Teaching in Higher Education*, 23(5), 576–92.

Rousseau, J.-J. (1762). *Emile*, London: Basic Books.

Royal Shakespeare Company. (2008). *Stand Up for Shakespeare*. Stratford Upon Avon: Royal Shakespeare Company.

Royal Shakespeare Company. (2010). *The RSC Shakespeare Toolkit for Teachers*, London: Bloomsbury Methuen Drama.

Ruiter, D. (ed.) (2020a). *The Arden Research Handbook of Shakespeare and Social Justice*, London: Bloomsbury Arden Shakespeare.

Ruiter, D. (2020b). This is real life: Shakespeare and social justice as a field of play. In D. Ruiter, ed., *The Arden Research Handbook of Shakespeare and Social Justice*, London: Bloomsbury, pp. 1–22.

Sahlberg, P. (2014). *Finnish Lessons 2.0: What Can the World Learn from Educational Change in Finland?*, New York: Teacher College Press.

Schechner, R. (2012). Play: The joker in the deck. In S. Brady, ed., *Performance Studies: An Introduction*, 3rd ed., London: Routledge, pp. 89–122.

Segal, L. (2017). *Radical Happiness: Moments of Collective Joy*, Brooklyn: Verso.

Semler, L. E. (2013). Emergence in ardenspace: Shakespeare pedagogy, *As You Like It*, and modus *If*erandi. In K. Flaherty, P. Gay & L. E. Semler, eds., *Teaching Shakespeare: Beyond the Centre: Australasian Perspectives*, Basingstoke: Palgrave Macmillan, pp. 97–110.

Sennett, R. (2012). *Together: The Rituals, Pleasures and Politics of Cooperation*, London: Penguin.

Shakespeare's Globe Theatre. (2020). 3rd Shakespeare and Race Festival. 26 July 2021, www.shakespearesglobe.com/seasons/shakespeare-and-race-2020/.

Shakespeare's Globe Theatre. (2021). Centre stage course. 24 July 2021, www.shakespearesglobe.com/learn/courses/centre-stage-course/.

Shakespeare Schools Festival. (2014). *2014 Workshop Notes*, London: Shakespeare School Festival.

Sharkey, J. (2004). Lives stories don't tell: Exploring the untold in autobiographies. *Curriculum Inquiry*, 34(4), 495–512.

Slade, P. (1954). *Child Drama*, London: University of London Press.

Sloan, C. (2018). Understanding spaces of potentiality in applied theatre. *Research in Drama Education: The Journal of Applied Theatre and Performance*, 23(4), 582–97.

Smith, E. (2019a). *This Is Shakespeare*, London: Pelican Books.

Smith, R. (2019b). Poverty and privilege: Shakespeare in the mountains. In S. O'Dair & T. Francisco, eds., *Shakespeare and the 99%: Literary Studies, the Profession, and the Production of Inequity*, Cham: Palgrave Macmillan, pp. 143–60.

Snyder-Young, D. (2013). *Theatre of Good Intentions: Challenges and Hopes for Theatre and Social Change*, Basingstoke: Palgrave Macmillan. https://doi.org/10.1080/13569783.2014.895626.

Soja, E. W. (1999). Thirdspace: Expanding the scope of the geographical imagination. In D. Massey, J. Allen & P. Sarre, eds., *Human Geography Today*, Malden: Blackwell, pp. 260–78.

Somers, J. (2013). Drama in schools: Making the educational and artistic argument for its inclusion, retention and development. *Drama: One Forum Many Voices*, 19(1), 5–12.

Stinson, M. (2009). 'Drama is like reversing everything': Intervention research as teacher professional development. *Research in Drama Education: The Journal of Applied Theatre and Performance*, 14(2), 225–43.

Stornaiuolo, A. & E. E. Thomas (2018). Restorying as political action: Authoring resistance through youth media arts. *Learning, Media and Technology*, 43(4), 345–58.

Stredder, J. (2004). *The North Face of Shakespeare: Activities for Teaching the Plays*, Exeter: Short Run Press.

Sutton-Smith, B. (ed.) (1979). *Play and Learning*, New York: Gardner Press.

Szabo-Cassella, C. (2016). *Shakespeare's Yoga: How the Bard Can Deepen Your Practice On and Off the Mat*, Ashland: White Cloud Press.

Tam, P. C. (2018). Teacher as fool: A study of the teacher's power in the carnivalesque practice of drama education. *Pedagogy, Culture & Society*, 26(2), 283–300.

Taylor, G. (1991). *Reinventing Shakespeare: A Cultural History, from the Restoration to the Present*, Oxford: Oxford University Press.

thisshaxisgay. (2020). A new podcast in which a director and a scholar explain why each and every Shakespeare play is a little bit queer. 18 June 2022, https://twitter.com/thisshaxisgay.

Thomas, E. E. & A. Stornaiuolo (2016). Restorying the self: Bending toward textual justice, 86(3), *Learning, Media and Technology*, 313–39.

Thomas, P. L. (2009). The futility and failure of flawed goals: Efficiency education as smoke and mirrors. *Power and Education*, 1(2), 214–25.

Thompson, A. (2011). *Passing Strange: Shakespeare, Race, and Contemporary America*, Oxford: Oxford University Press. https://doi.org/10.1093/acprof.

Thompson, A. & L. Turchi (2016). *Teaching Shakespeare with Purpose: A Student-Centred Approach*, London: Bloomsbury Arden Shakespeare.

Thompson, A. & L. Turchi (2020a). Active Shakespeare: A social justice framework. In D. Ruiter, ed., *The Arden Research Handbook of Shakespeare and Social Justice*, London: Bloomsbury, pp. 47–59.

Thompson, A. & L. Turchi (2020b). Shakespeare teachers' conversation: Teaching anti-racism through Shakespeare. 8 August 2020, www.youtube.com/watch?v=514eXyZ5kBo&feature=youtu.be.

Thomson, P. (2002). The comic actor and Shakespeare. In S. Wells & S. Stanton, eds., *The Cambridge Companion to Shakespeare on Stage*, Cambridge: Cambridge University Press, pp. 137–54.

Thomson, P., C. Hall, K. Jones & J. Sefton-Green (2012). The signature pedagogies project: Final report, London: Creativity, Culture and Education.

Thomson, P., C. Hall, D. Thomas, K. Jones & A. Franks (2010). *A Study of the Learning Performance Network an Education Programme of the Royal Shakespeare Company*, London: Creativity, Culture and Education.

Tickle, J. (2017). The theories of Lev Vygostsky as a framework for a critical analysis of learning during drama festivals organized by the International Schools Theatre Association (ISTA). *The International Schools Journal*, 37(1), 86–98.

Trilling, D. (2020). Why is the UK government suddenly targeting 'critical race theory'? *The Guardian*, 23 October. London. www.theguardian.com/commentisfree/2020/oct/23/uk-critical-race-theory-trump-conservatives-structural-inequality.

Tronto, J. C. (2017). *Who Cares? How to Reshape a Democratic Politics*, Ithaca: Cornell University Press.

Turner-King, R. (2018). Creating welcoming spaces in the city: Exploring the theory and practice of 'hospitality' in two regional theatres. *Research in Drama Education: The Journal of Applied Theatre and Performance*, 23(3), 421–37.

Turner, V. (1982). *From Ritual to Theatre: The Human Seriousness of Play*, New York: Performing Arts Journal.

Varaidzo. (2019). The 21st-Century Curriculum. *Seriously BBC Radio 4.* London, British Broadcasting Company.

Villanueva, C. & C. O'Sullivan (2020). Dramatic codifications: Possibilities and roadblocks for promoting critical reflection through drama in Chile. *Research in Drama Education*, 25(4), 526–42.

Vincent, J. (2016). Perspectives on love as a component of professional practice. *International Journal of Social Pedagogy*, 5(1), 6–21.

Vygotsky, L. S. (1978). *Mind in Society: The Development of Higher Psychological Processes*, Cambridge, MA: Harvard University Press.

Wales, P. (2009). Positioning the drama teacher: Exploring the power of identity in teaching practices. *Research in Drama Education: The Journal of Applied Theatre and Performance*, 14(2), 261–78.

Way, B. (1967). *Development Through Drama*, London: Longman.

Webb, D. (2013). Pedagogies of hope. *Studies in Philosophy and Education*, 32(4), 397–414.

Whitman, D. (2008). *Sweating the Small Stuff: Inner-City Schools and the New Paternalism*, Washington, DC: Thomas B. Fordham Institute.

Williams, N. (2018). Writing the collaborative process: Measure (still) for measure, Shakespeare, and rape culture. *PARtake: The Journal of Performance as Research*, 2(1), 1–20.

Wilson, R. (1997). NATO's pharmacy: Shakespeare by prescription. In J. J. Joughin, ed., *Shakespeare and National Culture*, Manchester: Manchester University Press, pp. 58–82.

Wink, J. (2011). *Critical Pedagogy: Notes from the Real World*, 4th ed., New Jersey: Pearson.

Winn, J. (2015). The co-operative university: Labour, property and pedagogy. *Power and Education*, 7(1), 39–55.

Winston, J. (2005). Between the aesthetic and the ethical: Analysing the tension at the heart of theatre in education. *Journal of Moral Education*, 34 (3), 309–23.

Winston, J. (2008). Beauty, laughter and the charming nature of drama. *National Drama Conference*, Durham. (Transcript of a keynote).

Winston, J. (2010). *Beauty and Education*, New York: Routledge.

Winston, J. (2013). 'Play is the thing!': Shakespeare, language play and drama pedagogy in the early years. *The Journal of Aesthetic Education*, 47(2), 1–15.

Winston, J. (2015). *Transforming the Teaching of Shakespeare with the Royal Shakespeare Company*, London: Bloomsbury.

Winston, J. & S. Strand (2013). Tapestry and the aesthetics of theatre in education as dialogic encounter and civil exchange. *Research in Drama Education: The Journal of Applied Theatre and Performance*, 18(1), 62–78.

Winston, J. & M. Tandy (2012). *Beginning Shakespeare 4–11*, London: Routledge.

Wright, A. (2012). Fantasies of empowerment: Mapping neoliberal discourse in the coalition government's schools policy. *Journal of Education Policy*, 27(3), 279–94.

Yosso, T. J. (2005). Whose culture has capital? A critical race theory discussion of community cultural wealth. *Race Ethnicity and Education*, 8(1), 69–91.

Cambridge Elements ☰

Shakespeare and Pedagogy

Liam E. Semler

University of Sydney

Liam E. Semler is Professor of Early Modern Literature in the
Department of English at the University of Sydney. He is author of
Teaching Shakespeare and Marlowe: Learning versus the System
(2013) and co-editor (with Kate Flaherty and Penny Gay) of
Teaching Shakespeare beyond the Centre: Australasian
Perspectives (2013). He is editor of Coriolanus: A Critical Reader
(2021) and co-editor (with Claire Hansen and Jackie Manuel) of
Reimagining Shakespeare Education: Teaching and Learning
through Collaboration (Cambridge, forthcoming). His most recent
book outside Shakespeare studies is The Early Modern Grotesque:
English Sources and Documents 1500–1700 (2019). Liam leads the
Better Strangers project which hosts the open-access Shakespeare
Reloaded website (shakespearereloaded.edu.au).

Gillian Woods

Birkbeck College, University of London

Gillian Woods is Reader in Renaissance Literature and Theatre at
Birkbeck College, University of London. She is the author of
Shakespeare's Unreformed Fictions (2013; joint winner of
Shakespeare's Globe Book Award), Romeo and Juliet: A Reader's
Guide to Essential Criticism (2012), and numerous articles about
Renaissance drama. She is the co-editor (with Sarah Dustagheer) of
Stage Directions and Shakespearean Theatre (2018). She is
currently working on a new edition of A Midsummer Night's

Dream for Cambridge University Press, as well as a
Leverhulme-funded monograph about Renaissance Theatricalities.
As founding director of the Shakespeare Teachers' Conversations,
she runs a seminar series that brings together university academics,
school teachers and educationalists from non-traditional sectors,
and she regularly runs workshops for schools.

ABOUT THE SERIES

The teaching and learning of Shakespeare around the world is
complex and changing. *Elements in Shakespeare and Pedagogy*
synthesises theory and practice, including provocative, original
pieces of research, as well as dynamic, practical engagements
with learning contexts.

Cambridge Elements ☰

Shakespeare and Pedagogy

ELEMENTS IN THE SERIES

Shakespeare and Virtual Reality
Edited by Stephen Wittek and David McInnis

Reading Shakespeare through Drama
Jane Coles and Maggie Pitfield

Podcasts and Feminist Shakespeare Pedagogy
Varsha Panjwani

Anti-Racist Shakespeare
Ambereen Dadabhoy and Nedda Mehdizadeh

Teaching Shakespeare and His Sisters: An Embodied Approach
Emma Whipday

Shakespeare and Place-Based Learning
Claire Hansen

Teaching with Interactive Shakespeare Editions
Laura B. Turchi

Critical Pedagogy and Active Approaches to Teaching Shakespeare
Jennifer Kitchen

A full series listing is available at: www.cambridge.org/ESPG

Printed in the United States
by Baker & Taylor Publisher Services